YOU CAN COMMUNICATE

PR SECRETS FOR PERSONAL SUCCESS

*Dedicated to the reader: You really can communicate.
And to Thérèse Bottomley for her wisdom and guidance.*

YOU CAN COMMUNICATE

PR SECRETS FOR PERSONAL SUCCESS

Stephen Manallack

Copyright © Pearson Education Australia Pty Limited 2002

Pearson Education Australia
Unit 4, Level 2
14 Aquatic Drive
Frenchs Forest NSW 2086

www.pearsoned.com.au

All rights reserved. Except under the conditions described in the Copyright Act 1968 of Australia and subsequent amendments, no part of this publication may be reproduced, stored in a retrieval system or transmitted in any form or by any means, electronic, mechanical, photocopying, recording or otherwise, without the prior permission of the copyright owner.

Commissioning Editor: Mark Stafford
Senior Project Editor: Carolyn Robson
Copy Editor: Susan Lee
Cover and internal design by Ingo Voss
Typeset by Midland Typesetters, Maryborough, Vic.

Printed in Malaysia

1 2 3 4 5 06 05 04 03 02

National Library of Australia
Cataloguing-in-Publication Data

Manallack, Stephen, 1947– .
You can communicate: PR secrets for personal success.

Includes index.
ISBN 1 74009 676 2.

1. Public relations. I. Title.

659.2

Every effort has been made to trace and acknowledge copyright. However, should any infringement have occurred, the publishers tender their apologies and invite copyright owners to contact them.

An imprint of Pearson Education Australia

CONTENTS

PART 1
Core lessons from corporate PR   1
1. How to get your message across   3
2. Learning from the best: finance   10
3. Barriers to communication   17
4. Learning from political leaders   28
5. Become your own PR department   34
6. Names, networking and getting ahead   41
7. Network for success   46

PART 2
Using communication to rise to your potential   51
8. Influencing bosses and making friends   53
9. Creating real communication   61
10. From pitfalls to promotion   66
11. Promotion and persuasion   75
12. Leadership is already within you   84

PART 3
Anger, crises, conflict and negotiation   89
13. Dealing with anger   91
14. Overcoming selfishness   101
15. Survival aids in a crisis   108
16. Communication breakdown and barriers   113
17. Handling conflict   119
18. Gaining influence through communication   125

PART 4
Presenting and selling   133
19. Successful presentations   135
20. Make meetings work for you   140
21. Surviving parties   146
22. Secrets of a good speech   150
23. Is the customer always right?   159
24. Think of the future as e-life   167

PART 5
Creativity and spirit: communicating for a better tomorrow   175
25. Communication and the human spirit   177
26. Some old-fashioned advice   185
27. You can be a creative communicator   190

INDEX   195

ACKNOWLEDGEMENTS

The author would like to acknowledge the following for extracts reproduced in this book.

Elizabeth Foley, Elizabeth Foley & Associates (pp. 46, 47). Reprinted with kind permission.

Harvard Business School Publishing Corporation (pp. 115, 122). Reprinted by permission of *Harvard Management Communication Letter*, from 'Handling Conflict in Teams' (April 2000), and 'Communication Breakdown' (September 2000). Copyright © 2000 by Harvard Business School Publishing Corporation; all rights reserved.

Hodder Headline (p. 53). Reprinted with permission from *The Art of Happiness* by the Dalai Lama, 1998.

Dr William J. McEwen and The Gallup Organization (p. 161). Reprinted with permission from the *Gallup Management Journal*.

Penguin Australia Ltd (pp. 47, 48). Reprinted with kind permission from *The Women's Power Handbook* by Joan Kirner and Moira Rayner © 1999.

Kevin Roberts, Saatchi & Saatchi Australia (pp. 37, 48, 49, 180). Reprinted with permission.

Sandra Yates, Saatchi & Saatchi Australia (pp. 63, 178, 179). Reprinted with permission from 'Reinventing Conversation'.

PART 1

Core lessons from corporate PR

1 How to get your message across 3
2 Learning from the best: finance 10
3 Barriers to communication 17
4 Learning from political leaders 28
5 Become your own PR department 34
6 Names, networking and getting ahead 41
7 Network for success 46

HOW TO GET YOUR MESSAGE ACROSS

LEARNING FROM CORPORATE PR

Can you learn better personal communication by studying how corporations get their message across? Before I decided to write this book, a friend asked me to help him get his message across—he was after a promotion. My first response was, 'I help corporations to communicate, not people'. I had not realised that corporate PR had so much to teach the individual.

My friend suffered from a fear of communication. His big concern was appearing foolish by saying the wrong thing at the wrong time. He had no confidence in either his timing or his delivery. The more we talked, the more we realised that how corporations communicate holds secrets for how you can get your message across, relate to people and get ahead. Corporate communication particularly holds valuable clues for people who are shy or have a fear of communication, which of course leads to communication failure. I told my friend that corporations with good communication were successful corporations because they were happy with themselves, good places to work and had bright futures. The more they communicated, the happier they were. The happier they were, the better they communicated. Better communication may even make you happier, too.

Can successful corporations provide lessons for our personal lives? The answer is a definite 'Yes'.

The first lesson from corporations with good communication is this: they have a clear idea of who they are and where they are going. By knowing themselves, they are less fearful about competition and can create a strong brand. They spend a lot of money developing and promoting statements about themselves, such as vision statements, mission statements, positioning statements and other themes. Consistency of message is a real aim of corporate communication. This avoids chaotic communication and keeps everyone to the same message. You will perform better as a communicator (and the psychologists tell us you will be much happier), if first you understand yourself. Take a look inside and be happy with what you see.

> *You will perform better as a communicator . . . if first you understand yourself.*

Second, these companies know they need lots of friends in the form of suppliers, customers, employees, advisors, legislators and more. They are not islands. To meet and keep corporate friends, they communicate a lot.

While corporations need lots of friends, they accept that they need some more than others. When Telstra decided to move the mobile telephone network from the old analogue network to new technology (CDMA network), it divided its target audience (friends) into primary and secondary. That is, in getting this message across, some parts of the audience were more important. For example, because of rural sensitivity and high influence among politicians, a primary audience included farmers, the fishing industry and the mining industry. Of secondary importance were the media, the regulators and the political parties. This distinction, put in place by Telstra and its PR consultants Turnbull Porter Novelli, meant that Telstra put more communication effort into getting the message out to farmers than it did communicating with, say, suburban shopkeepers. Applying this in your personal life, you will focus more on the people who really matter to you, instead of being diverted by people on the fringes of your life and work. A father who spends evenings down at the pub with some mates and not at home with his children has not followed the corporate lesson of segmenting your friends, and spending more effort on those who matter the most. As a result of not making the distinction, his communication breaks down and relationships suffer. Making the right choice early about who matters most can avoid the pain of failed relationships.

You, like a corporation, are not an island. You will certainly perform better if you accept that your personal satisfaction and future prospects are dependent on those around you. It's useful to think that you need others more than they need you. This can be a humbling thought. Even the rich and famous depend on others: to make their champagne, drive their limousines, create the latest fashions and so on. Someone has to make or create everything that we tend to take for granted. So it is good to realise your dependence on others. The alternatives are confusion and loneliness. Many confused and lonely people show, under testing, that they do not like themselves. To create good communication, first learn how to get on with yourself, be nice to yourself and like yourself more each day. Liking yourself means you will get on better (communicate better) with the people who matter to you.

> **To create good communication, first learn how to get on with yourself...**

The third key lesson is that successful organisations constantly worry about what others think of them. We call this being concerned with perceptions. By being 'worried' about what other people think I mean having a healthy level of interest and concern. This is not negative in the way that fear is, because fear stops you communicating. These companies have a real interest in people, and in satisfying some particular need or service for people. This does not make them clingy or neurotic, but it does mean they accept that what people think about them is as important as what the organisation actually does. This view has been around for a while: the ancient Greek philosopher Epictetus said, 'People are disturbed not by things, but by their view of things'. Successful organisations constantly find out what people think of them. Communication experts call this market research.

Market research works well for corporations. Individuals, whether seeking to climb the career ladder or to improve their relationships, will also do better by applying their own market research. This involves being interested in others, listening closely, enjoying people, finding out what they think and asking questions. This inquiring mindset will help you overcome fear. The idea that having a strong interest in others will help you to promote yourself is foreign to many 'get-ahead' books, but it's true for many of our best corporations and can work for you.

Modern corporations are increasingly being told to love their customers and cherish their partnerships. A good way to evaluate your performance here is to ask: do I really like the people I live with, work with and deal with? If the answer is 'No', you have found the fundamental reason for your own poor communication. We do not communicate well with people we do not like. This can only be turned around by changing your own attitude (not by changing others) so that you learn to like people.

Fourth, good organisations know that everything they do has an impact on how they are perceived. They know that if they cheat in one part of their business, the whole business is at risk. They know that if their talk is not matched by action, they will soon be disbelieved. Their corporate image is underpinned by their belief that everything they do or say is important. Cheating and gossiping are not part of the corporate plan, and this kind of negative action and talking will not help you communicate either. In fact, cheating and gossiping are often the major causes of personal communication breakdown.

Taking the earlier corporate example of Telstra changing the network for mobile phones, the company and its PR advisers, Turnbull Porter Novelli, decided strategically that it was important to provide tangible evidence that the new technology was best suited to Australia. Sure, it had extensive research and references from leading world authorities, but that was not enough to win the communication task. So using the media as a conduit, they created a series of major testing programs in regional locations where the media could test the equipment. That is, by being open and throwing everything under the spotlight of the media, they communicated tangible proof that the change of network was needed. In this, their performance matched their image, creating successful communication. For you, the concept of tangibility provides a challenge. It is one thing to say you care about something or someone, and quite another thing to actually show it by doing something. Only when you add action to words are you believed.

Good corporations believe that everything they say and do matters. Isn't this also true in your daily life? Your action, or inaction, impacts on how your friends feel about you and on your career reputation. You can't say one thing but do another without people noticing.

Don't expect to become an instant success at communication. Corporations have learnt that quick fixes are no fix at all, and they build patience and the long term into their communication programs. As the fluctuations of communication occur, it is best to accept that you will never achieve a smooth state of perfection in your communication with others. Sometimes you will do brilliantly, while at other times perform so poorly that others wonder if you have really tried. These fluctuations are inevitable. By understanding how corporations have solved communication problems, you can gain a better understanding of your communication strengths and weaknesses, and correct the downswings that occur.

> **You can't say one thing but do another without people noticing.**

Even our best communicators will sometimes find themselves issuing confusing signals or being indirect or a little uncertain. If you find yourself doing this, don't be too self-critical and give it all away, believing you can never conquer communication. It is not a matter of conquering, it is more a matter of knowing where you are in communication and then taking steps to improve your position. Instead of thinking 'I was a bit deceitful there, I am so hopeless', by skillful monitoring you will think 'I was a bit deceitful there, but now that I have noticed it I can move on to more accurate and factual communication'.

Translating these corporate PR techniques to your own communication, you will be a better communicator if you:

- Get to know yourself first and be comfortable and happy with who you are and where you are going.
- Decide who are the people that really matter to you, since you are not an island and do need others, and if necessary change your attitudes so that you really like these people.
- Observe what these people think (in general, on a specific topic and about you) and communicate to change inaccurate perceptions.
- Accept that what you say and how you act should be the same, because there are real communication dangers in saying one thing but doing another.

My friend (the one seeking promotion) later told me he was grateful for the communication techniques, but he had a lingering problem: prior to any interview, he perspired a lot because he visualised the interviewer as an aggressive, tough person and himself as a quivering mass of failure. This was a vivid and painful thought in his head. This 'monkey mind' caused him real pain. While not preventing him using the newly acquired skills of communication, the fear would certainly make him perform below his best.

We discussed how most of our sporting heroes today are using visualisation to improve their performance. A basketballer, for example, will visualise shooting baskets or dodging the opposition. So, we practised alternative visualisation: changing a bad mental image into a good one. He started with the interviewer. My friend closed his eyes and visualised his closest loved one. He then visualised the interviewer, but before the negatives chipped in, he visualised this interviewer transforming into the image of his closest loved one. Gradually, the fear reduced. Then, my friend was able to extend the process: to picture the interviewer as a child, growing up, making and losing friends, having dreams and building a family. In this way, he realised the interviewer was a person just like him, not someone to be afraid of. Importantly, by visualising this his mind became implanted with the positive image. He did not get rid of the monkey mind, but he did create a mental alternative. By combining this mindfulness with his new communication techniques, his career went ahead.

LESSONS FROM 'THE FOUNDER OF PR'

Most of us in corporate PR refer at some time to 'the founder of PR', Edward L. Bernays, who was Sigmund Freud's nephew. Based in the USA, Bernays drew from Freud's insights into the human mind and created campaigns to change the taste or desires of the public. His career spanned the 1920s through to the 1970s and his clients included Proctor & Gamble, the Russian Ballet and politicians such as Herbert Hoover. One example of his work was helping Simon & Schuster sell books by convincing architects that every quality home should have built-in bookshelves. He was one of the first to create 'impartial' committees or boards to provide 'expertise' and 'independent commentary' on subjects of interest to his clients, and these so-called independent groups were funded by his clients. Today he would be a controversial figure, and some of his techniques may no longer be acceptable. But he had a great capacity to influence public opinion and get his clients' messages across. How did he do it?

Know your audience and tailor the message to them

Nowadays, it is commonplace for political candidates to analyse their electorates, gathering information about people's ethnic, educational, economic and political backgrounds so they can carefully craft their messages to suit each group. Successful marketers of products and services do the same. Bernays pioneered this technique in a New York mayoral election in 1940.

Cultivate influential people

Bernays was a role model for his ability to build strong relationships with influential people. These included media, celebrities, experts and politicians—basically anyone who could help him promote his clients.

Be prepared to sell an idea on a different basis

Much of the work of Bernays seems to predate the concept of lateral thinking, which was so successfully developed by Edward de Bono in the later part of last century. Consider the earlier example of the bookshelves, which people then needed to fill with books.

Choose the right timing

A good message delivered at the wrong time dies a quick death. Bernays knew that the Sunday papers were news packed, so he directed clients away from them. He even advised a Czech nationalist leader to hold off a declaration of freedom from the Austro-Hungarian empire from the proposed Saturday to the next day so the news would be prominent in Monday's press.

Get to the point and be memorable

The Multiple Sclerosis Society wanted Bernays to help raise awareness of this appalling disease. He advised them to shorten the name of the disease to MS, which was much easier for the public to say and to remember.

Get others to communicate your message

In his time, Bernays used independent groups, celebrities, politicians and experts to lend credibility to his clients' causes. To add spice to the dour image of President Calvin Coolidge, Bernays arranged for a trainload of Hollywood celebrities to visit the White House. When the bacon industry suffered from the trend to faster breakfasts, he arranged public messages from doctors, reinforcing the importance of eating a good meal at the start of the day.

Try, try again

Bernays knew that if a cause failed initially, time could ultimately be on its side.

For the corporations that hired Bernays, these communication tips worked wonders; they can work for you too. While you may see his approach as manipulative, there is a little bit of manipulation in every bit of personal communication, even in its most pure form. 'I love you' and 'Please help me' sound heart-rending and pure, but they are designed to gain a reaction, to manipulate. Communication is not a neutral act; it aims for a result. So why be squeamish about deliberately using communication to get what you want?

Almost all of Bernays's techniques can be applied to your personal communication. Most modern corporations, often without knowing it, use some or all of his approaches. However, instinctively many of us resist his approaches. Many think that cultivating key people is humiliating, too contrived or crawling. Others want to be blunt with their message, rather than think of alternative ways (such as the bookshelves) to get it across. I have also seen many people stubbornly push certain messages even when they acknowledge that the timing was wrong. Basically, it is your choice.

I have seen people who, although brought up the hard way, living off the streets and being virtually unemployable and by many standards 'unlovely', have built new friendships, gained jobs and developed some happiness, largely through learning how to communicate. If your communication has broken down, it is never too late to recommunicate and reconnect. Surely communication and fear of others should no longer hold back your relationships or your career.

> *... there is a little bit of manipulation in every bit of personal communication ...*

2 LEARNING FROM THE BEST: FINANCE

HOW THE FINANCE SECTOR PROMOTES ITSELF

The fastest growing, most dynamic business sector of the last few decades has been finance. Whereas once we might have looked to car manufacturers, paper makers, food processors or large-scale building companies for insights into modern communication, today the best, most innovative communication is coming from finance. When it comes to borrowing from the strategies of the corporate world, why not start with the most successful sector: finance? Your personal communication will improve if you learn how finance goes about getting its message across. Finance covers banking, stockbroking, investment education, insurance, financial planning, credit unions and more. These fast-growing firms dominate every modern city. Finance is on our TVs, in our magazines, on billboards and provides the brightest lights on our tallest buildings. What can you learn from finance? What communication secrets have made it a leading growth sector?

Mostly you see these financial giants via their advertising: the bright red diamond shapes of HSBC, the blue square and back slash of Deutsche Bank, the clean no-nonsense look of Credit Suisse, the rich marble tones of Citigroup and the rampaging bull of Merrill Lynch. But it is below the advertising that the real communication happens for these financial giants. They know that their success depends on relationships, on people. Communication holds the key to their success. It holds the key to your success too. This 'below the advertising' world of marketing and communication can be tough. It calls for the hard slog, but it pays off. It is where real communication occurs, after the glossy advertising has created a general awareness and credibility. Tops in this slogging world of personal contacts and face-to-face marketing are the growing armies of financial planners, working with clients to build and manage wealth.

> **They know that their success depends on relationships, on people.**

Why is communication so important to financial planners? Some of the best financial planners spend as much as half their time and a quarter of their income on business development (another phrase meaning communication). That is, for every hour they spend with a paying client, they should be spending an unpaid hour out there, communicating with the prospective client. Or for every $100 they earn, $25 never makes it into their pocket because it needs to go straight back into more communication. That's how important communication is. It explains why this finance sector has seen astronomical growth, and why it stands out for those of you who want to learn about communication.

Most financial planners will say their best new business comes from referrals; clients are sent to them by related companies, friends, clients, contacts or centres of advice. Put that way, it sounds fairly inactive. You could be fooled into thinking that referrals are things you just sit in the office and wait for. Forget it; people who sit and wait end up sitting and waiting. Referrals for new business come from careful communication and hard work. How financial planners get referrals can guide you in how to communicate.

I think the most satisfying form of referral for anyone in the business of giving advice is the one that comes from an existing client. When one of your clients sends a friend along, it is high praise indeed. Most financial planners would agree. This process begins with being good at your job. You can forget communicating for success if you are not prepared to be the best in the business and competent in all skill aspects of your career, whether it is plumbing, banking, marketing, selling, consulting or any other field.

> *. . . people who sit and wait end up sitting and waiting.*

Referrals do not come just because you have done a good job; people need to know that you have done a good job, and that knowledge comes from communication. For financial planners, this means not only creating a great plan for the client, but also communicating that plan to the client. They sell the benefits and communicate their concern and dedication to the client. This communication is reinforced at critical times, such as when news hits about a new stock float or the market judders up or down. Good planners take time to phone their key clients for a reassuring chat at times of high client interest in their own money. It's time-consuming communication, but it pays off in client loyalty and in referrals. Thinking about others (the clients) works well in finance and it is the key to good personal communication for you.

In the bid to gain more referrals, the best planners are aware of centres of influence and cultivate these via good communication. What is a centre of influence? It may be an association for employees or a social club. It could be six or seven of the best clients, who are well respected and sought out for advice. It may be a community group or political leader. For some, it may be a media commentator. It could be a charity or a good cause, supported by leading lights in a particular field. You can find centres of influence at the opera or the football; they could be in local government, in the medical association or in the school alumni group. They are anywhere that people may talk to each other about you and your field. To play a role in (exploit) these centres of influence, you need to get out of the office chair and become involved. Take a committee position, attend meetings, forget the TV and dedicate some nights to good causes or fun events. Centres of influence never work for couch potatoes; they work for people who are prepared to be active and to have a go. Centres of influence work for people in finance; they can work for any aspect of our lives.

Sometimes you will need to think creatively to make communication work for you. One financial planner thought outside the square with a promotion for a carpet cleaning business. What has carpet cleaning got to do with financial planning? The owner of the business was a client of the financial planner. For one month, the planner let it be known that any new client would receive carpet cleaning free of charge (that is, paid for by the planner). This was good for the planner, good for his carpet cleaning client and good for newcomers. In almost any activity you can duplicate this form of creative thinking and energetic communication. Think about who you could team up with. It's a matter of thinking smarter about your business and the people you serve. Which of your current contacts could become a valued partner in an initiative like the carpet cleaning example?

> ... get out of the office chair and become involved.

SEVEN TECHNIQUES YOU SHOULD BE USING

Most financial planning firms have seven techniques in their marketing and communication programs. Each of these has relevance to your own communication. These successful financial planning communication techniques are:

- Cultivate centres of influence.
- Conduct and attend workshops and seminars.
- Write articles and appear in the media.
- Correspond regularly with clients.
- Attend conferences and trade shows.
- Create a buzz around your results.
- Take courses to improve personal communication.

Each of the seven strategies contains secrets for those who want to improve communication, develop themselves as a brand and be more successful.

Cultivate centres of influence

Busy, successful people are good networkers, and networking is at the heart of cultivating centres of influence. Think of the individuals most important to you, and develop a plan to communicate regularly with them. As you complete a course of study, keep in touch with those lecturers who have the best reputations. When you are moved within the company, keep contact with former colleagues who are also on the way up. Phone people, write a letter, attend meetings, get out there. Think of the groups or associations that matter to your client prospects, and become involved in them. Analyse your friends, contacts, work colleagues, existing clients or other businesses and work out who you can usefully team up with. Start by recording how much TV you watch each week; then decide to cut it by 50 per cent and use the extra time on networking. You'll enjoy yourself more, and success will follow.

The key lesson here is to make note of the people or organisations who are most important to you. These people and organisations should receive most of your attention and most of your time. Too many of us waste time and energy on the small and insignificant parts of our day, but when you have created a list of the most important, you can make sure your time and energy is rewarded.

> *Phone people, write a letter, attend meetings, get out there.*

Conduct and attend workshops and seminars

I've been to some hopeless seminars that would have bored people and driven them away. Seminars and workshops can work hard for any communicator, but you have to work hard to be successful in them. It starts with the planning: finding the right timing and the right topic for the target audience. That is, you need to listen to people and ask questions so you know what is on their mind. This is almost a first law of effective communication. It is also important to decide who you want to attend, and then work hard to get them along. This is not just a matter of sending out invitations and waiting for responses; you need to be on the phone, getting out there and convincing people to attend. Then the key is to create presentations that satisfy the audience while strengthening your brand. Use their language, include some surprises and keep it short, easy and fun. The top financial planning firms may put on fifty or more workshops, seminars or conferences every year; year after year. They are scared of being seen as just a commodity and want to become a real person, so the effort on speaking and meeting people pays off.

To get ahead, make a practice of attending meetings and seminars in your area of work or in your community. Become involved; start slowly, by asking the occasional question or making a short comment. Be prepared before you go. Gradually, you will become a better participant, and you will be meeting with more of the people who matter to you.

Write articles and appear in the media

You may *say* you are good, but when others tell me you are good I am really impressed. See the difference? When an independent third party endorses you, it has credibility. I can confidently take action on that endorsement. Independent third-party endorsement is what any media appearance offers people wanting to succeed in their career or in their business. The good news is that in almost every area of endeavour, the media is hungry for stories and copy. Find the right publication and provide them with good written material and you have started on the road to gaining strong, independent third-party endorsement for your skills.

Dominic Alafaci was named Financial Planner of the Year by *Money Management* magazine in 2001. With a track record of accounting and financial stints with Deutsche Bank and HSBC, he now runs Collins House Financial Services, a financial planning firm. He is a busy man, with a young family and many calls on his time. His involvement in sport and the community is just another draw on his valuable time. Despite the pressures, every Monday Dominic leaves the office and puts on headphones at a leading radio studio to talk money with the host and callers. This takes a lot of time and preparation. It also saps energy. Since he is already the Financial Planner of the Year, why do it? Dominic knows that communication is a total package, and to work well it needs everything going for it. Sure, he is successful because of attitude, skills, contacts, seminars, direct mail and referrals, but profile plays a role too. That is why he slogs it out on the radio every week.

Listeners are aware that he never directly promotes himself on air; the messages are all about shopping around and seeking lots of advice. This is the key to his credibility, and I have seen him repeat the same message in his office, inviting people to talk with competitors and gain a broader view. He believes in what he and his industry are doing.

To get on air he had to be involved, because it is the Financial Planning Association (FPA) that first nominated him for the radio slot. Previously, he had been involved in the FPA and was an active participant and willing speaker. He had filled speaking spots for them at short notice and done the right thing. When there was an opportunity for media training, he took it. In doing so, he became a natural choice for radio. He's a good example of doing a bit of everything in order to win new business, because these days you can never be sure why people chose you over a competitor. In this environment, he rightly focuses much of his leadership energy on communication.

Correspond regularly with clients

What is the forgotten communication tool of the last few decades? It is undoubtedly the letter. Easy to do, high in impact, memorable, effective but often overlooked, the art of letter writing will help you advance your career or business. To succeed with letters you need to write well and to send them on a regular basis. Email, which I would include in the term 'letters', is leading more of us to start written communication again. It is improving human communication, so use emails. Someone once told me early in my business years that if the only piece of paper the client receives each month is your invoice, it stands out too much and may actually be read closely! Cynical perhaps, but containing a truth that if we neglect people they neglect us. The lesson for those wanting to advance in their careers is that they should regularly use the written word to communicate with people who matter. Written communications do not replace other means (such as conversations, meetings and presentations) but they are another valuable way of keeping communication going.

> *... if we neglect people they neglect us.*

Attend conferences and trade shows

Every area of life has its own culture. This culture is most clearly seen when people hold meetings, conferences and trade shows. Conferences and trade shows are like tribal events. To succeed, you need to be a part of the culture. At the same time, you need to be apart from the culture. It is a fine balancing act. Attend the important functions held in your particular field (your culture) but make sure that you use each of these to reinforce your point of difference, your brand edge over all the competition.

Those who get too carried away with these tribal cultural activities are the ones who attend absolutely everything, stay till well past the end, find a comfortable seat at the bar and seem to never want to go back to work. This is overdosing on tribalism. Remember that you need to be a part of whatever culture you are in, but that you also need to demonstrate how you are apart from it. Otherwise you are just another number, another anonymous part of the tribal cast.

Create a buzz around your results

In modern communication, it does not pay to be shy. It does not pay to hide your light or be too modest about success. We are all busy; there are many calls on our time and attention. So when you have grabbed our attention make sure you use this valuable time to reinforce your achievements.

One financial planner I know always seemed too low key. On meeting, his response on how business was going was to mumble 'OK' and then start talking about some other area of business where people made a killing with no effort. There was never any buzz. He could easily have created that buzz by taking one simple step that would work for you: always prepare an answer to that question 'How are you going?'. Incorporate an easy statistic on client growth, or put in a few success points. Being prepared is how good communicators create a 'spontaneous' buzz. For example, when someone asks 'How are you?' you should never answer with something like: 'Oh, I think I'm OK. Yeah, not bad thanks'. This is a wasted communication opportunity, for instead of creating a buzz you have started a snooze. It's boring and noncommittal, and most of us talk this way too much of the time. It is better to have some highlights (personal, business or professional) that you can leave the other person with. That way the communication has worked for you, instead of vaguely against you.

> Being prepared is how good communicators create a 'spontaneous' buzz

Take courses to improve personal communication

The good news about the art of communication is that it is a skill you can learn. Most born communicators have been made; they have attended communication skills courses. Seek out courses on better writing, improved personal communication, speechmaking and media appearance. Almost any course will add new depth and power to your personal communication, so when the chance of attending courses comes your way, be the first to say 'Yes'.

The modern finance sector oozes success and reeks of communication. Study it, and you will improve your communication. While the tip of the iceberg for finance is the bright lights on buildings and the glossy advertising on TV and in print, the real hard work of communication for finance happens at street level, where people meet people and do business together. It is a timely reminder that communication is an individual endeavour, and that to succeed you have to act.

BARRIERS TO COMMUNICATION 3

Don't be afraid of ideas that are contrary to present practice. Most everyone who gets to the top gets there for doing something different.
Arthur W. Page, one of the pioneers of corporate PR, 1935

THE POWER OF THE MIND

Which part of the body plays the most important role in communication? Is it the eyes? Perhaps it is the voice and the mouth? Or the clothes we wear? Could it be the way we stand, or the gestures we use—the body language? It's actually none of these, although each of them plays a role in getting the message across. The part of the body holding the key to success or failure in communication is the mind. Corporations understand this well. They know that the strength of their messages is not found in their advertising, on billboards or on their website; the real strength of any corporate communication can be found in the 'corporate mind', in the value and integrity of what it does to build relationships. The secret of effective communication for you is also in the mind, coming from a combination of attitude and skills. If you know how to do it, and your mind wants to do it, you will succeed. If, on the other hand, your mind wants it but you have no skills, your efforts will miss the mark, just as you will also miss if you have lots of skill but an unruly mind telling you that failure is at hand.

OVERCOMING THE COMMUNICATION DIVIDE

Corporations spent billions of dollars last century refining the art of communication, creating a flowering of mass communication. They learnt how to get the message across. Mass communication created 'Diamonds are forever' for de Beers and saw the creation of global brands, such as Coca-Cola, through 'Coke adds life' and 'Coke is it'. In the last few decades of last century, global communication built McDonald's into a household name and launched Merrill Lynch (bulls and bears) as a financial powerhouse. In all these cases, love them or hate them, we knew what each company provided, what they stood for and what they meant to us. The communication was clean and effective.

Not so effective is the communication between individuals. Too many people are left at the bottom or middle level of their organisations purely because their communication skills are not good enough to earn them promotion. This is a waste of talent, as well as a frustration for the individual. At the end of the century that saw the emergence of mass communication, as individuals it seems many of us lost the art of talking. As companies spent billions of dollars studying the art of communication, we forgot the old skills that created real communication. We forgot how to create understanding and cooperation between people. As technology allowed for instant global communication if we want, when we want, many of us became more lonely and isolated. People became increasingly tongue-tied. As a generation learned to use the Internet, providing instant global access and communication, they did not learn how to communicate one to one, within households and communities.

Unfortunately, today we suffer from a communication divide. Communication has the greatest capacity to unite and build friendships, but it seems that today we use communication more for negative than for positive outcomes. For example, studies have shown that people today criticise thirty-three times more frequently than they compliment. We have refined the art of complaint and lost the art of friendship and support. When you say 'They never tell me when I do something right but they always tell me when I do something wrong', it is actually true. We are using communication as a negative weapon more often than we use it to build bridges. We are also creating divides by not communicating; fewer people today know or speak to their neighbours. As a result, there is less real community.

> **We forget how to create understanding and cooperation between people.**

The good news is that the lessons so well learned and so skillfully applied by corporations last century can be relearned by individuals in this. We can regain the art of communicating, enhancing our careers and gaining more success. We can learn communication from those corporations that are good at it.

Communication is a two-part process for corporations. The most successful corporations know that first they need to have the product or service right, have it available and reliable, before they communicate. Only when the full delivery of the product or service is in place do they build the message through mass communication. Learning from this, as individuals we need to mirror corporate experience and create a two-part approach, gaining the skills of better communication and building the right mental attitude.

Corporations face the communication divide, especially those who are slow to respond to change. Many corporations that grew in the era when profits were the sole objective have been slow to change as our communities have become concerned with environmental and ethical issues. This has created a communication divide, further expanded by forces against globalisation. The divide comes about because too many companies have been out of step with consumers. They have not kept up with change. When facing these barriers to communication, global PR consultancy Hill and Knowlton has been pushing its corporate clients to move towards green and ethical standards, claiming these are good for communication and good for business. Greg Ray, the Australian Managing Director of Hill and Knowlton, told members of the Australian Institute of Company Directors:

> To be included in an ethical fund means there must be genuine substance to a company's corporate conduct. This usually means the company, for example, has a published corporate environmental policy, it communicates environmental issues with stakeholders, and it runs an employee environmental program. Importantly, this approach can foster an internal, ethical culture. Employees at all levels start to participate and contribute and it begins to feed on itself. The new culture can boost employee satisfaction and pride. It can foster increased quality, performance and productivity and it can build bridges between employees and management through a spirit of common purpose. In short, it can be extremely good for business.

In convincing companies to change and to accept that being green and ethical makes good business sense, this PR firm has a systematic approach. We can learn from this as we, too, face constant change and need to modify our communication to meet new circumstances in our lives.

The vulnerability audit

The company takes a 360-degree view and identifies those areas where it is particularly vulnerable. As Greg Ray says, this 'is often a very sobering exercise'. The key is that once a company fully understands the risks and the barriers to communication, it can set about fixing things up and getting the message across. So much of corporate communication begins with honest self-assessment, and this should be a starting point for you.

The decision

The next step in this corporate process is to make a decision to change, to become a green company. Having faced up to vulnerabilities, the board of the company makes the decision to change how it operates. Following this example in our daily lives means we look at ourselves, identify weaknesses and problems, and then make a decision to change. Without the decision, it is all just navel gazing and the barriers to communication remain in place.

Establishing a policy

This is where the company puts its decision into words. These words should be simple and inspirational. They 'sell' the new approach, gaining understanding and support for it. This applies to each of us when we set out to change things. We need to find the right words and use them to overcome barriers and build trust. But be warned—Hill and Knowlton warn their corporate clients: 'abuse that trust and you will live to rue the day, because you will be punished severely'. In other words, you have to mean what you say.

Setting the benchmark

This is where the company can see if it is being successful or not. It might set a benchmark of getting the new message across to, say, 80 per cent of customers. It's the same as making a personal commitment to get on better with our family, build bridges at work, team up with everyone at the club or have a chat to the neighbours. Decide to do it, then do it.

Selling the new image

Companies know that there is little point to change unless people know about the change. Perception is everything. Ethical and environmental policy changes need to be communicated and any program for getting this message across would address management, employees, customers, suppliers, governments, fund managers and more. One successful example has been a major mining company, WMC (Western Mining Corporation), that was among the first to produce an annual Environmental Report. The whole purpose was to be transparent in an area where many kept things well away from the public gaze. This brave communication strategy was a matter of meeting things head on and being open and honest: not bad advice for personal communication.

One final tip from Hill and Knowlton when you face a communication breakdown or crisis: they tell their corporate clients 'never, never lie or try to cover up the truth'. If this is good enough for corporations, surely it is good enough for you.

KNOW THE BARRIERS TO COMMUNICATION

As the art of corporate PR developed last century, we gained knowledge of the main barriers to communication, and most of this knowledge has only been available to corporations. Now this knowledge can help you overcome fear. The word 'communication' is from the Latin *communis*, meaning common. The purpose of communication is therefore to establish commonness with others. The other side of the coin is communication breakdown. Communication can break down for a variety of reasons, but the most frequent barriers to getting the message across are:

- Delivering a good message at the wrong time, for example when the other person is flustered or preoccupied. These messages are never understood.
- Expressing the message badly, such as rambling or being confusing. These messages hardly ever get across.

- Not waiting until you have the listener's attention. Poor attention creates poor retention.
- Jumping to conclusions. This is what happens when 'premature evaluation' takes place. You should watch for this, because when it occurs people often jump the wrong way.
- Being fearful, combined with lacking trust and respect, blocks communication.

To overcome these barriers start by studying the communication behaviour of companies that succeed. What do these successful companies do in their communication? They take an interest in people all the time so that their communication messages get across. They are totally focused on what people think, but when they find that people don't like them or their product, they don't go and hide. Instead, they start planning ways to make people take another look, to begin a new relationship. By market research (which is a practical and positive way of being worried about what people think) they find the best way to get their message across. Then they go in to action, confident that they have the story in which the market will be interested.

Better communication is all about choice. You can choose success by building positive communication habits, using the secrets of corporate PR. If you want more success in business or personal life, then take steps towards better communication. But you are unlikely to take steps towards better communication if you have no understanding of how communication works. Unfortunately, most people have been told communication is something you are born with; we hear of the born communicator and the person with the gift of the gab. In my experience of working with dozens of senior corporate leaders, most became good communicators through training and practice. I cannot think of one who would qualify as a born communicator. Another misleading view is that improvement and progress occur in a straight line, despite the reality that communication is much more chaotic than that. It fluctuates wildly, confusing us and alienating our friends and colleagues. But we can improve our communication performance and outcomes if we understand how corporations communicate, applying their secrets to our lives, our company or our community.

> *. . . most became good communicators through training and practice.*

WHY DOES COMMUNICATION SCARE US?

Communication either confuses or scares most people. Yet if we cannot make ourselves understood, how will we be happy and get ahead? We are scared of communication because few of us received any communication training at school or university, and those of us who did get some training often found it too theoretical and unhelpful. It is ironic that, in a modern high-technology society, where all the communication systems are available to us, few of us have learned about how to get our messages across. We have placed the focus on the medium, neglecting the messages.

Ignorance breeds fear. Many potentially good communicators are unnecessarily fearful, purely because they remain ignorant of communication skills. Even those working in communication fields, such as advertising and PR, often do not know which communication techniques work or why something they did works. Most see communication progressing in a straight line: think about communicating, set a strategy, create the messages and success should be a smooth trip. They are surprised when the straight line is interrupted, when communication fails to get the message across.

Understanding corporate communication can remove many of your fears about personal communication. Just as people who have a huge fear of flying can learn to overcome it by gaining a close appreciation of how the aircraft works, so you will reduce your fear by learning how communication works. Ignorance causes fear; knowledge increases confidence.

Corporations never take communication for granted. They may be the best in their field, but they know that they still have to work hard to get this positive message across. Too many corporations have failed to gain market share because, despite their product being top quality, people had a perception that some other company made a better product. That is, they failed because of perception, not because of their product. Being the best, and making sure people know it, is a common corporate mission. Despite this experience, one of the great misconceptions of modern times is that if you know your subject, you can get it across.

> *. . . they failed because of perception, not because of their product.*

Some of those who are experts in their field are hopelessly tongue-tied when it comes to communicating about it. Even at family functions, the uncle who knows the entire family tree becomes a stumbling, mumbling wreck when called upon to speak about it. Knowing a subject and communicating a subject are two different things. Certainly, credible communication is based on knowing your subject, but this alone is no guarantee of getting the message across.

The good news is that almost everyone can learn how to communicate: fortune does favour the brave. You can improve communcation and therefore add value to relationships and build your career. You can fast track your communication learning by studying how corporations go about the task. Even the most fearful can make forward steps along the positive communication path. I have experienced this. Starting out as a shy person, I developed a career where I have helped organisations and senior executives communicate and get their messages across, with confidence and impact. Because I started out on the shy side, I have learnt many lessons about effective communication and these can work for you too. Many of the business executives who seem to be accomplished public speakers and good communicators are often also very shy. They decided to learn how to communicate, knowing how important it is in success.

Good corporations work hard to raise the self-esteem of their key people, ensuring that they have a positive awareness of how good the corporation is. You can easily apply this tip: just by liking yourself a little more, you are more interesting and valued. Feel that way, and somehow your communication works. Corporations conduct regular communication reviews to see how things are going. You can do this too. Every now and then, look inside yourself and try to feel what the mind is seeing there. Perhaps there is a quiet fear, a sense of failure or even a dislike of aspects of yourself. By going inside and seeing these fears and feelings, you have begun on the road to getting on top of them. Without this, you will never understand why your communication is so poor. The key lesson from corporations is that to achieve good communication with others, you must have a good relationship with yourself.

OVERCOMING YOUR FEARS

The key question is: are we ready to start relearning how to communicate? When the skills are missing, something will move in to take their place and, for many of us, that something is fear. While fear is there, we are not ready to communicate. We are afraid to communicate because our mind tells us it will not work. Yes, the corporate communication skills so finely tuned last century can be a guide for each one of us. Skills are the first part of a communication renaissance. The mind is the second part.

> *While fear is there, we are not ready to communicate.*

Communication skills will not work if you do not take steps to control the monkey mind that produces negative thoughts. Remember that the mind plays a huge part in communication failure. If you struggle with fearful thoughts before meetings, parties, visiting friends or just going out, in addition to learning new skills from corporate communications you will need to overcome this fear.

All of us have some level of what is called the monkey mind. This is the mind that is all over the place, constantly chattering and jumping about, never moving straight ahead, fearful of obstacles and dodging at shadows. Look at it this way: isn't it just a part of life that our mind is variable, given that some scientists believe we have as many as 70 000 thoughts every day? The mind does a staggering amount of thinking, and plenty of this must be complete nonsense. This monkey mind is the origin of the fear that stops us reaching our full human potential. It shows up in isolation, fear, shyness, failure, withdrawal, anger and frustration. In many of us it is so powerful that we just accept these as part of life or as our lot in life. But I know we can overcome the results of the monkey mind.

A positive attitude provides you with a good communication launching pad; just as a positive business approach launches good corporate communication. Instead of having that monkey mind chattering away, causing you to imagine the worst, if you can begin to see things as they really are you will be more assured and take better steps to open communication. Then you become more open and friendly, as the need to be closed and fearful disappears.

During my school years I was so shy and afraid of communicating that many of my school friends now wonder how my career ever led me to PR consulting. I spent a lot of time in the negative part of my mind, letting its fearfulness and chattering stand between me and effective communication. Perhaps knowing the other side of the coin allowed me to become a better communication adviser. Of course, I was not the only shy person at school. Although at the time, my monkey mind convinced me this was so. At a recent school reunion, I concluded that as many as 50 per cent of my classmates suffered from stunted communication at school, partly due to shyness. Perhaps the entire class had it at some level. All that varied was the degree to which shyness interfered with fun, growth and learning.

My own brand of shyness was accompanied by a desire for success and acceptance, so a constant tug of war was going on inside. 'Stay out of the limelight' was one voice inside of me, while 'Get in there and have a go' was the other. The result was often a disastrous combination of the two. For example, I had a fear of debating and public speaking, but joined the debating team. There my shyness took over and I often sat mute and embarrassed, hoping others would do all the talking. The constant fears magnifying in my monkey mind were 'Are they all looking at me' and 'What will they think of me?'. In class I knew the answer to most of my teachers' questions but was too shy to speak up, or so shy when asked that I confused the issue or gave half the answer. Under the intense red heat that shy people experience, speaking up became a jumbled communication.

My school memories include the many times when communication could have made me new friends, or made better friends of acquaintances, but shyness and fear intervened. It was like a full circle. I was truly the victim of my own preoccupation with myself.

Today, with this experience of shyness combined with my knowledge of communication, I am making a call to be brave: do not let a fear of what people think stop you from communicating. In my role as a PR consultant, I have worked with the most nervous and shy executives, helping them lift their communication effectiveness. In my experience, born communicators are made, most having started poorly but learning new skills to get the message across. The ones who progressed were prepared to have a go. They overcame the chattering mind. If you always anticipate what people will think, you will stunt your own growth. You will be too scared to do anything important. On the other hand, by maintaining a healthy interest in people, and a concern for what they think, you can build a strong platform for ongoing communication and relationship growth. Fear is the road to failure; communication is the highway to success.

Just as corporations know their success comes from engagement with customers, so getting involved with people is an essential first step towards your success. Fear will leave you feeling miserable. A strong fear of what people think will stop you gaining that promotion, making that sale, joining that sporting club or taking that course. It will keep you off that committee, stop you saying 'Hello' to colleagues or neighbours, prevent you from applying for that promotion and make you reject that invitation to a morning coffee club. Fear prevents us from getting involved with people. A little fear is natural, so when it comes just note that fear is there, but then go forward. Don't let it stop you. Everybody feels this level of fear at some time, but successful people do not give in to it.

> *In my experience, born communicators are made . . .*

A psychologist friend provided one explanation for extreme shyness: the shy person is too frightened to say anything because what others will see may not match the person's self-image. He believes shy people have big egos. So big that they are fearful of exposing them to any form of damage. The shy person chooses to share nothing and risk nothing. Perhaps this explanation is a bit harsh, but there could be some truth in it. For most of us, who have some degree of shyness, the message here is to be prepared to take the risk, because the alternative is to stand still.

> *Fear prevents us from getting involved with people.*

One of the pioneers of the PR profession was Arthur W. Page, who became the first Vice-President of PR for AT&T. Page was not afraid of controversial communication methods, nor was he fearful of controversial subjects. In 1949, Page helped organise the National Committee for a Free Europe, aimed at foiling the growth of communism and promoting democracy in Eastern Europe. He was certainly ahead of his time, yet he faced many critics and could have given in to a fear of criticism or failure. He did not give in. His approach when confronted provides lessons for us all. Plenty of people attacked this committee as a CIA front and so on, and prominent among these was a syndicated columnist and radio personality, Fulton Lewis Jr. Lewis claimed that the entire committee was a group of 'misguided souls'. Instead of retaliating (as many of us might have), instead of becoming indignant and aggressive, Page simply offered to provide Lewis with any information he wanted about the group and even offered to meet him at any time, any place to discuss any aspect of the committee. This positive response largely disarmed his opponent. It must have been tempting for Page to list all the facts, to fight back with the positive achievements, to go on the front foot and specifically respond to the negative points of Lewis. Instead, he offered complete openness, in one simple way showing that the negative views were hollow. This form of openness succeeded for Page and can work for you, becoming a real personal communication asset, replacing fighting with talking, and fear with cooperation.

One of the best creative directors in my advertising agency used to say to clients, particularly to new clients, 'Safe messages are boring'. Companies that deliver safe messages, without risking high creativity and energy, generate very little interest. The communication fails. The creative director was preparing them for the courage needed to deliver good advertising, which means creative advertising. I have been in boardrooms where senior executives have rejected advertising messages that they acknowledge were terrific ('That is the best message I have seen. I love it, but is it going to . . . ?'). They did not have the courage to accept good communication. Fear prevented them from using inspirational messages and great communication. It takes courage to stick your neck out; it takes nothing to be ignored.

Many people have successfully used visualisation to overcome fear. Most of our sporting heroes use visualisation all the time; prior to games or contests they visualise themselves performing well. We need to build visualisation into other areas of life, including business communication. Before you go to a meeting or party, close your eyes, breathe slowly for a while and, when your mind is at rest, start to create mental pictures of everyone who will be there. Then picture yourself with some of these people. See yourself with a smile, moving through the groups with an open face, nodding to friends and smiling at people you do not know. Picture yourself moving forward to a group of people you have never met. Feel their warmth and interest floating towards you. Feel that you genuinely like these people, and they like you.

The head of a major engineering consulting firm had to overcome strong fear of social occasions and, to his credit, got to the top of his organisation. Some of his tips for overcoming fear have stuck in my mind and may help you:

- When joining a new group or committee, don't expect instant happiness and instant friendship. You may feel a little alone for several meetings. Be patient.
- Present yourself and your ideas in an open way, rather than starting a conversation with emphatic 'I don't like . . .' statements.
- Commit to avoiding any disagreement with, or avoid suggesting changes to, the group until you are a comfortable and accepted part of it.
- Be flexible while you find out what people are really like. The person who seemed like someone you would hate can later turn out to be your best friend.

He became a wonderful mentor for young engineers joining the firm and had the knack of bringing out the best in people who had begun as poor and fearful communicators. As you tackle the twin keys to successful communication—the mind and the technique—two of his words will have real meaning for many aspects of your life and for your improving communication: 'Be patient'.

 LEARNING FROM POLITICAL LEADERS

At least once every four years, citizens of the USA are given a huge reminder of the important role communication and image play in leadership. What has this got to do with learning from corporate communication? The best senior executives that I know have all been keen to learn. They have spent time analysing what other leaders do and say. Ray, the CEO of a mid-size fund manager, once confided in me that he spent a lot of time studying political speeches and election campaigns. He picked up lots of tips for his own communication. Of course, Ray did not tell any of his colleagues this for fear of being laughed at or being dubbed 'the candidate'. But that did not stop him improving his own communication by keeping an eye on politicians' techniques.

> **The best senior executives that I know have all been keen to learn.**

Elections are about communication, and candidates use a multitude of strategies and techniques to promote themselves. It's all about generating the right image. At election time, communication becomes the key. If you want to learn some new skills for getting your message across and advancing your career, it pays to study the way political leaders have gone about the task.

Do you think you couldn't learn anything from a politician? With such a closed mind, promotion could pass you by. We can all learn from each other, including from those in the tough world of politics. Those who can particularly learn from some of these political techniques are people who:

- excel at making things add up, but aren't seen to add value
- are tops at keeping information, but rarely use it
- become the best keeper of information and the worst communicator of messages
- have the finest brain for complexity and the worst for simplicity
- show patience with detail and impatience with generalisation
- focus on the specific and fail at the big-picture messages.

You may not be running for high office, but you can learn some new communication skills from those who do, so that your important messages do get across.

THE 'LINE OF THE DAY'

Every morning, communication professionals and other strategists in the White House meet and agree what message the President and the President's hundreds of support staff should emphasise. Once agreed, that 'line of the day' is repeated by press secretaries in press briefings, issued in writing, handed out by others in the executive and used as often as possible by all at the White House. This stops communication becoming sidetracked and ensures that almost all the media have the same take, or angle, on the White House. After all, if the only thing the media get from the White House is the line of the day, what else can they use?

President Ronald Reagan was often called 'The Great Communicator' for good reasons. Looking back, most Americans remember his eight years in office as a time of strong economic growth and of the collapse of the Berlin Wall, with the eventual fall of communism in that region. Few cite the Iran Contra Affair in 1986 when the USA had secretly sold arms to Iran. Yet this could have blown up. But Reagan ran a tight media team, faced the media and confirmed the facts. He appointed a review board, allowed his personal staff to testify, brought in new people with reputations for ethics and set the scene so that, by the time he gave a speech of contrition, the public had plenty of reasons to believe he had changed. Reagan was a committed line of the day leader, not afraid to repeat messages until they had sunk in. But he also knew words need the support of action and so he strengthened the ethical base of his team.

> **Action plus communication make a powerful defensive combination.**

This reinforces an ethical message we deliver regularly to corporate clients: 'You can't carve rotten wood'. If the corporation is not good, it is impossible to generate good communication. It was the same for Reagan; without real action his line of the day would have gained little or no credibility and the problem would have grown. Action plus communication make a powerful defensive combination.

What does this line of the day approach mean for the individual? For most of us, it would be too structured and clinical to have a line of the day. But it serves to remind us that sometimes we need to stick to a message and say it often so we can be sure we get the message across. At work this may mean presenting a point of view at a meeting,

> **...we need to stick to a message and say it often...**

repeating it to the boss, sending it to others in a memo and discussing it in the canteen. To get the message across, you may need the patience to go through this process more than once. Without patience and repetition, your communication can miss the point.

This line of the day approach can work in the office when friends and colleagues ask, 'How are you going?'. Too often we provide a mumbled response of no consequence. Answers such as 'not too bad' or 'OK thanks' fail to communicate much at all, and can actually leave a negative impression. If, on the other hand, you have some issue, point of view, proposal or topic on your mind, then this can become your line of the day and provides a really positive answer to that 'how are you going' question. This can provide a small but significant improvement in your image.

SETTING THE AGENDA

Once political leaders would only communicate when they had made a decision. Today, government communication is more strategic and much of it paves the way for later decisions. This is called 'setting the agenda' and can be a useful approach at home and at work. If there is something you want or a decision you need, instead of asking for it straight away, start a discussion around the topic and keep it going. Then make the move to take action or ask for the decision you want. People are more prepared, and you will be more likely to get a favourable response, if you follow the lead of political leaders in setting the agenda. An example may be that the Prime Minister has plans to fund programs for homeless youth. Instead of announcing these immediately, almost out of the blue we will see the Prime Minister visiting with homeless youth, holding a national talkfest and inviting selected young people to Parliament House. Then, when the momentum has been built, the Prime Minister will announce funding for programs for homeless youth.

> ... start a discussion around the topic and keep it going.

> ... it is not always best to ask straight away for what you want.

In personal life, one message to take out of setting the agenda is that it is not always best to ask straight away for what you want. Sometimes you need to set the scene, or get people ready for the request. This may appear to be too manipulative for you. Although life is a process of change, many of us adopt a mental attitude of clinging to the way things are and we fight any change. That is one reason why your apparently reasonable requests can be denied. So it is wise to consider our allergic reaction to change, and set the scene for it before making your move.

CONTROLLING THE INFORMATION FLOW

Political leaders seem to the public to come in and out of the media spotlight. Few realise that this is part of their strategy to control the flow of information to the media. Sometimes they will resort to a constant flow, to wear the media down. At other times they seem invisible, but this adds huge interest and weight to their next media appearance. On slow media weekends, they will choose to make a statement on some issue that is of less media appeal, but will get a good run because there is not much else happening.

For you, controlling the information flow can help you get the message across by finding the right time for the right statement. Our minds are impatient to make a point, even when we know the other person is less receptive at that time. By fighting the mental impulse to blurt it all out you can wait for the right time for the few well-chosen words. You will also avoid becoming the bore, who never knows when it is time to leave a topic alone.

USING MEDIA TRAINING TIPS

Many times it looks as though politicians have never had real media training. In press conferences, the untrained ones seem to be under siege and ramble a lot, leaving us all feeling very unconfident and uncertain. Some of these media training tips would help politicians and others under intense questioning:

- Pause before you answer.
- Keep answers short.
- Don't speculate.
- If a question is tough, ask a question.
- Close answers with a pleasant smile.
- Think of the reporter as your favourite uncle or auntie.
- Emphasise and re-emphasise points.
- Show compassion and concern.
- Stay on the record.
- Remember that the interview is never over.

You can use these techniques in the office or in meetings, to improve the quality and clarity of your responses. It's better than later thinking of what you would have said, had you given yourself time to think.

CONTROLLING STRESS

One of my tennis partners, Sonia, was chatting off court about the previous evening's pre-election debate on TV. She was stunned by how the Prime Minister seemed so calm in the midst of a storm. 'How do they do it?' was her frustrated question. Sonia had many experiences where her own stress levels came between her and getting the message across. She was too tense, too quick, too jumpy ever to create real communication.

Life often leads to this level of stress for all of us, and as the level rises our communication effectiveness declines. There are some simple strategies for changing this negative stress into positive communication, and although I don't know for certain that political leaders use these techniques, I am pretty confident they do, particularly in the confines of their office. From this list, you can choose the ones that work best for you. The whole purpose is to find a way to control the stress levels so that you can get your message across.

- Make time in your life to be alone, listen to your mind, check your intentions and calmly think about where you are going.
- Plan to do something that is just for you, that you really love, each day.
- When you face what seems to be a huge problem, talk it over with someone you trust.
- Get out and take a walk; make your lungs work.
- Say 'No' when asked to do something that you really do not want to do. But say it politely.
- Simplify your life, starting with the trivia that can drive your day.
- Sit still, listen to your breathing and feel happy to be alive.

One of my bosses from early in my career had a fabulous piece of advice for those difficult tasks: 'Remember, it takes less energy to get an unpleasant task done right away than to worry about it all day'.

SEND CLEAR, POWERFUL MESSAGES

In my analysis of what works in communication, there is no doubt that through history the best political leaders have excelled in creating messages. Candidates who never made it to the top office generally failed because their messages were confused, they didn't appear honest, they talked in riddles or we just were not sure what they stood for. These candidates had no chance. But all successful political leaders have created clear, simple messages that hit the mark, repeated the story and projected honesty. This is a powerful recipe for your communication success.

Any part of your life where getting your message across is important (that's probably every part of your life) can be improved by an honest evaluation of how your messages perform. Are they, for example, clear and simple or confusing and detailed? Do you repeat certain core messages or are you always jumping all over the place? Have your messages hit the mark or do they leave others unsure of who the messages are for? The more you succeed at creating messages, the greater will be the power of your communication. For many, shifting to positive communication creates the first time in which they are really understood by those around them. For them, transforming their messages has transformed their life.

Why are presidential speeches so powerful? How do they work so well at getting people on side, even those who don't want to agree? You can learn persuasive communication techniques from virtually any presidential speech and it pays to read a few to see how they work. I have studied presidential speechmaking from President John F. Kennedy through to George W. Bush. Most of their speeches simply state what they want the audience to do or to believe, and then provide all the reasons why they should. This simple two-step approach can work in any communication situation where you want people to support you. Good speakers let the audience know up front where the speech is going, and they have also thought about who the audience is and what their hot buttons are. By telling people at the outset what the President wants them to do or believe, there is little chance of misinterpretation of their message. Having told people what they want them to think, feel or do, these good speeches then sell the benefit of making that move. They address the 'what's in it for me?' question, and you can do this too if you think first about what your target audience is interested in. One of the common mistakes we ordinary beings make is to go into huge detail on the features of something and never get to the real benefit of it. That's like telling me my computer has XYZ zillion megabytes of ABC—all gobbledegook to me—when all I really want is the benefit of instant access to the Internet. Go to the benefit first, and only use detail if you need it.

> *. . . think first about what your target audience is interested in.*

On top of this two-part approach (tell them what you want them to do and explain the benefits in their language) the good presidential communicators exude trustworthiness, honesty and competence. No matter how much pressure they may be under, they stay relaxed and in control of themselves.

So, whether you are asking the boss for a raise or presenting to the local community group, take some tips from 'the President':

- Think about what the audience wants to hear.
- Let them know where you are going and what you want.
- Explain the benefits to them.
- Speak with confidence.

Love them or hate them, US Presidents include some of the world's best political communicators. While they tread a global stage, their techniques and 'tricks of the trade' can help you in most aspects of daily communication. Who knows, you may even win a vote or two.

5 BECOME YOUR OWN PR DEPARTMENT

Corporations know that individuals are the best communicators. That's great news for you, because it means many of their secrets are about how to get individuals out there and communicating. Study and imitate what they do, and you will be on the way to becoming your own PR department.

While corporations spend a fortune on advertising, they also make sure that all their employees understand the corporate message. They place special training emphasis on any of their people who meet with customers. They do this because every communication technique, including advertising and direct mail, is only a poor substitute for face-to-face communication.

PUT ON A HAPPY FACE

As a corporate communication adviser, I have developed many training programs to ensure that staff became good ambassadors. One of the quirky aspects of this work is that while few of these corporations have spoken in terms of happiness or happy messages, these are the true and often intangible benefits of having individual people spreading the message for you. Happy messages work this way: if someone likes their work, it shows in happier communication, reflecting well on the corporation. Think about it; we prefer to talk with somebody who smiles and laughs readily and is interested and enthusiastic. This form of communication creates a bright face for an otherwise faceless organisation. To put corporate tips to work for you, first you will have to lighten up and brighten up: as mum used to say, 'Put on a happy face'.

> *... if someone likes their work, it shows in happier communication ...*

Successful organisations are comfortable with themselves, which means they like their staff. They regard their whole staff as 'the PR department', knowing that everything they do, big or small, impacts on the organisation's reputation.

I experienced an example of this when telephoning to cancel an appointment with a physiotherapist. The physio had been treating a sore shoulder, caused by years of hitting the tennis ball the wrong way. Her receptionist did the obvious: she straight away pinned me down to another appointment time. Was this good PR? No, this was just good commonsense business service. The good PR occurred when the receptionist said: 'Can you tell me how your shoulder is? The physio will want to know'. Now that is doing the extra bit, showing concern and communicating well with your target audience. You could increase your PR effectiveness simply by following the receptionist's example and being interested in other people. That receptionist was acting as the physiotherapist's PR department, and was therefore worth her weight in gold.

You are your own PR department. Let's face it, nobody else is going to do your PR for you. To be your own PR department means accepting that your relationship and promotion opportunities depend on your own communication efforts. The good news about this is that we are all fascinated by people. Despite what you may think, the people you want to impress are already interested in you. It's just a matter of giving them reasons to like you or promote you. You'll do even better at this if you are happy and interested in yourself too.

To fully appreciate the role happiness plays in communication, take a moment to evaluate yourself. If you are feeling desperate, focusing just on yourself and feeling you have missed out, then you will probably say on a regular basis, 'People don't understand me'. Just as companies with infighting and unhappiness fail in the marketplace, unhappy people create poor communication. On the other hand, if you have most of what you want, think a lot of other people and have some sense of achievement, then you probably find that people do understand you. The happier you are, the better you will be at getting the message across. The better you are at getting your message across, the happier you will be. One of the most important aspects of communication is to think a lot of other people and to be genuinely interested in them. Good corporations do the same.

> ... the people you want to impress are already interested in you.

THE FIVE-STAGE ADOPTION PROCESS

Follow the lead of good corporations: excel at listening and asking questions; speak in language people can understand; be enthusiastic and positive; repeat important points; and, thereby, never leave your reputation to chance. Corporations know that sometimes you have to be patient because it can take a while for people to adopt new ideas or accept new products. Most corporations work on a five-stage adoption process:

- **Awareness.** A person becomes aware of the idea or a new product, often by means of an advertisement or a news story. At a personal level, you can make them aware of your new ideas with a brief

comment, an action or leaving a book on the topic lying around.
- **Interest.** The person seeks more information about the idea or the product. In a commercial environment, they ask for a brochure, pick up a pamphlet, read an article or drop in to the store. At a personal level, they may ask you a question about your new idea.
- **Evaluation.** The person evaluates the idea or product on the basis of how it meets specific needs and wants. Feedback from friends is part of this process. At a personal level, they may discuss your new idea with some friends.
- **Trial.** The person tries the product or idea on an experimental basis, by using a sample, witnessing a demonstration or making some qualified statements on the topic. In personal communication, they may come back to you with, 'I was reading an article about your idea and . . .'.
- **Adoption.** The person begins to use the idea or product. At this stage they may make declarations of belief or support for your idea.

These five stages are not a set rule, they don't take a set amount of time and the whole passage is fairly unpredictable. After all, we are talking about people here. But they do provide a useful tool for understanding the steps most of us follow. Sometimes we can go through all five stages in almost an instant, while at other times we dwell on it for months. This process highlights the importance of continuous communication.

With communication comes freedom: freedom to be yourself, to express yourself fully and to reach your goals.

BUILDING YOUR BRAND EDGE

Aren't people cynical these days? Rightly so, perhaps you are saying. We do not trust big government, have little respect for business and more than 70 per cent of us do not care for advertising. We are looking instead for the human touch. Too many marketers have forgotten one simple truth: human communication is one of our greatest needs. Forget this need and your relationships or career will stall.

Against this growth in cynicism, good corporations strive to create a brand image that lasts and lasts. This brand becomes a real asset for them. Consider yourself as a brand. How can corporate knowledge of brand advantage help you communicate your own brand?

If this sounds a bit clinical to you, remember that brand advantage does not come from super sales pitches or motivational hoopla, it comes when your target market believes the brand:

- listens to them and cares for them
- reliably delivers what it promises
- is always interesting by being different or innovative

- wraps up any dealings smoothly and simply
- is happy, and projects this happiness.

These are great human values, and they underpin most of today's successful commercial brands. Your own communication will improve if you ask more questions and listen more closely. From then on, be more forthcoming about yourself, while more interested in others. This balancing act is difficult, but it reaps rewards.

There are some shocking new four-letter words emerging when the corporate world meets to discuss the future of brands. Of these words, the least used up to now in the corporate world and therefore the most surprising to hear, is 'love'. Corporate marketers are being urged to remember the power of love in their brands. It was in the 1960s that The Beatles sang 'All you need is love' and now brand managers are starting to believe it. The global advertising firm Saatchi & Saatchi has been urging marketers to spend less time concerned with respect for their brand and more time with love for it. Most marketers work hard building respect, and spend no time creating love for their brands. They use TV as an example of a brand that took over; in 1950 there was a TV in only 9 per cent of households and by 1960 (that's just ten years) 87 per cent of households had TV. Today TV is everywhere. They point out that people love TV, and they hate TV, but they do not respect it. They love it, hate it, but above all watch it. Corporate executives are being reminded that human beings think with feeling and emotion. Further, emotion is built into every decision we make. Kevin Roberts, Saatchi's global CEO, sums it up for his corporate audience:

> *Corporate marketers are being urged to remember the power of love . . .*

> *I've been standing up in front of business audiences, technology audiences, advertising audiences, and I've been talking about love. And I have survived! Love can be taken seriously. Love does matter. Love does have power. What does this mean to you? To win, to thrive in the coming decades you must look past the old brand battles and aspire to a Lovemark.*

One of the brightest accounting experts took years and years to make it to partner, because he thought it was enough to be technically brilliant. But he was introverted, did not laugh very much and was generally regarded as being miserable. There was never a sign of emotion, enthusiasm, passion or personality in his communication. Inside, he was actually quite happy, so the task was to learn how to laugh out loud, relax in public and communicate his happiness. His partners wanted more of this human side before they would accept him into their ranks. Only by learning how to communicate did he finally make it into that elite group. His communication course paid off.

Research has shown that when businesses lose customers, 70 per cent are lost because they do not like the human side of doing business with that organisation. This finding can provide the key to your own relationships and career success: through better communication, you can build your human side (your brand) and get on better. But to build your brand, whether as a business or as a person, you first have to make some decisions:

- What do I want others to know about me?
- What do I want to keep to myself?
- What do I want to limit to select people or groups?
- How many of my attitudes will I open up about?

Answering these questions with thought and honesty may just surprise you. It will guide you to an understanding of your own brand, and how you can strengthen it.

WRITING FOR THE RESPONSE YOU WANT

Does your written communication fail to get the response you want? One reason for this failure is that many of us project two personalities: at the personal level, we are fun and interesting, while when sending letters we become formal, dull and boring. Poor writing ultimately costs sales, business or friends.

Why is so much written communication stiff and formal?

Thinking too much about writing can hurt. Just get on with it, is a good maxim. But some thinking can help you write in more interesting ways. Ten points to help you improve your writing are:

- Think about who you are writing to (Where are they? What are they interested in? How do they know you? What do they want?).
- Based on what you know about them, create a shopping list of points for them.
- Write by linking these points together, from most to least important.
- As you are writing, feel as if you really like the person to whom you are writing, even if you do not know them well.
- Open your written message with a bang (grab them) or something familiar that everybody can agree with.
- Write clearly and simply.
- Use short words and avoid jargon.
- Vary the length of your sentences.
- Be passionate about your point of view, service or product.
- Ask the reader to take specific action.

Of the ten points in the list, the two that matter most in a business or sales letter are to think about who you are writing to and to ask them to take specific action. The first point (think about them) is critical to establishing the relevance of your service or product. If you are writing about the newest range of mountain bikes, don't babble on about the features of the bike, but instead explain how it will solve their business and sales problems. The tenth point (ask for action) makes them take notice and not chuck the letter out straight away.

If you can't open with a bang, a good replacement is to open with a question. We like to be asked questions. It shows the writer is interested in us.

You can learn writing skills from some of the best corporate advertising. Creative writing teams know that the mind learns by building on what it already knows, and so they begin their advertisements with the familiar and lead to the product or service they're selling. This can work in your writing. For example, instead of writing 'This collapse in value of dot com companies is the biggest since the massive depression of the 1920s' it is better to start with the familiar: 'Since the massive depression of the 1920s, the biggest fall has been the collapse of dot com companies'. The second version works because we see something we are familiar with first and it leads to the main point.

Familiar words and phrases will help improve your written messages. There's nothing special in the words of Bob Hope, and their very ordinariness and familiarity add to the impact of his 'If you can fake sincerity, then you've got it made'. It's lively, but simple.

After all that, if your writing still seems stuffy, be a bit adventurous and put in some provocative points or leading questions. And hold strongly to this core belief: dull written communication will let you down, so avoid it at all cost.

Try getting started on a writing task with this thought in your mind: I like myself, and I like the person I am writing to. It will make your words more personal and less formal. Personal writing is powerful communication.

CHIPPING AWAY AT THE COMMUNICATION BLOCK

Communication gives us the freedom to be ourselves and reach our goals. Sadly, for most of us, there is a blockage keeping us from ever finding that real freedom. This communication block consists of all the things that keep us from expressing ourselves and from really listening to others. The most common elements inside the block are fear, poor self-esteem and low interest in others. Most of us have a bit of one or two of these in us, at some stage in our life.

To gain the freedom to achieve your dreams, start by getting rid of the communication block. It is not easy, the block is rarely ever totally removed and sometimes it grows back. But while the block is in charge, you are less than you. You achieve less than you should. You fail. This is ultimately not your failure; it is the failure of the communication block.

The block keeps thousands of highly skilled people from being promoted. It stalls careers that would otherwise flourish. The key to overcoming the block is do not attack or blame yourself. Instead, get to work on that communication block. Freedom is communication; communication is freedom. The block is all that comes between you, freedom and communication.

The best ways to chip away at the communication block, from my experience working with successful corporations and corporate executives, are to:

- **Recognise it.** When your mind says 'Don't say hello', that is the block, not you, speaking.
- **Be inquisitive.** Ask questions because every question reduces the block, which relies heavily on ignorance and inaction.
- **Clarify your view of yourself.** Write down all the positive things about you. This could include something as small as having donated some old clothes to the Salvation Army. This will create a more positive self-image. The block works on negatives; it hates positives.
- **Appreciate and like people.** Decide that other people are important to your happiness and decide to like people. Approach them with a warm and friendly attitude, even when the block is trying to tell you that these people will not like you.
- **Value your friends and be patient.** Don't become too ambitious for a whole group of new friends. Place value on the ones you already have and develop new friendships slowly. This is how corporations treat their customers. Communicating well with existing customers is rule number one.

> But while the block is in charge, you are less than you.

Having seen the desperate attempts of homeless and drug-affected young people to learn how to communicate—in some cases in order to save their lives—I wonder why so many people in the middle of good careers, with lots of opportunities, can't do the same. Of course, they can.

NAMES, NETWORKING AND GETTING AHEAD 6

Isn't it embarrassing when you know someone's face but can't remember their name? It is not only embarrassing, it creates a barrier between you and them. They could interpret it as a deliberate put-down or as an indication that you don't care about them or don't find them interesting. They may even conclude that you are aloof and cold. This barrier will stop you making good friends, getting ahead and getting your message across. Forgetting names can be costly because, deep down, people do not like to be forgotten.

Corporations know that if people forget the name of their product, sales will drop. That's why they repeat the name so often, in all forms of promotion. You can learn to use this repetition too. Corporations also know the importance of the human touch, and most train their sales and customer service people in the art of remembering and using names.

> **Corporations know that if people forget the name of their product, sales will drop.**

As a corporate communicator, I have seen the best senior executives work the room at functions and conferences, addressing everyone they meet by name. People react well to this; they love to be acknowledged. It is insulting to be forgotten.

Dale Carnegie placed a lot of focus on getting names right in his landmark book, *How to Win Friends and Influence People*. One of his quotes highlights the importance of names: 'Remember that a person's name is to that person the sweetest and most important sound in any language'.

One of the secrets of the best corporate leaders is that they have a genuine interest in others. If you are consistently forgetting names, perhaps you are not happy with yourself or have little real interest in others. In my observations among corporate leaders, happiness with oneself and interest in others are two traits that go hand in hand. You can't have one without the other.

> **...happiness with oneself and interest in others are two traits that go hand in hand.**

Change your attitude to one of intense interest and liking of people, and you may remember names much more easily.

Techniques to help you remember names

Many successful corporate leaders have systems to help them with names and memory, such as keeping cards recording information about people. They record when they last met, who their family is, their favourite sports and so on. They refer to these cards before functions. Finding out who will be attending also improves their chance of putting names to faces.

As soon as you are introduced to a person, say their name out loud, early and often. This will help it to lodge in your brain. When you first meet someone, try saying something like: 'Nice to meet you, Steve. So, Steve, what do you do?' Using the person's name twice works far better on the memory than just saying: 'Nice to meet you. What do you do?'.

It all starts with paying close attention when introduced to someone, and even making sure that you know the pronunciation of their name. If you've heard the name and can pronounce it, you have a better chance of remembering it. Ask for the name to be repeated, if necessary. Early on, most people don't mind being asked: 'Would you mind repeating your name? I didn't catch it'. Some people tell me it helps to repeat the name many times to themselves, though I think once or twice using the name in conversation works much better.

If you have forgotten a name, own up to it: 'I'm sorry, I've got a mental block on your name and I should know it'. This is a much better approach than that of the so-called wit who tries to bluff his way out of it by saying: 'I've always been fascinated to know the exact spelling of your surname' only to find it was Smith or Jones!

Then there is the memory technique of visualisation. If we associate a person's name in our mind with some aspect of their features—and really concentrate on the visualisation—then we remember the name. It doesn't work for everyone, but it's worth a try.

The key steps for remembering names are:

- Decide to like people a lot.
- Use the name out loud in conversation as early as possible.
- Make sure you can pronounce their name properly.
- Ask the person to repeat their name if necessary.
- Repeat the name to yourself.
- Visually associate the name with some strong feature of the person.

The most important of these is to use the person's name in your conversation, early and often. It will generally stick in your mind.

TIPS FOR NETWORKING

Remembering names is just one part of being successful at networking. If, for example, you are one of those people who at a function always looks over the shoulder of the person you are talking to, you are actually hurting yourself. Networking goes beyond simply remembering names; you also have to be interested in people. Looking over somebody's shoulder makes you look desperate and unhappy and is insulting to the person in front of you. It tells the person you are speaking to, in a powerful way, that you would rather be talking with someone else. One of the most successful politicians was famous for the capacity to talk to one person, focusing totally on them, in a room of hundreds of people. He was seen as caring and interested.

Networking is the hot topic of the last decade, with every corporate leader trying to gain new skills. People flocked to training courses to learn how to network. Of course, like most aspects of communication, networking is not new and it is hardly rocket science. Yet many of us have no idea how to network. Like forgetting names, being unable to network will impact negatively on your life and career, so it is worth picking up some of the basics. If you take a positive and deliberate approach to networking, you will find that this extra level of concentration makes it easier to remember names.

My seven tips for networking are a compilation of observations of the best corporate networkers, the leaders who really know how to work a room and make an impact at any event.

> *. . . being unable to network will impact negatively on your life and career . . .*

Focus, focus, focus

When you first start talking to someone, whether an old friend or someone you have just met, concentrate your focus totally on them. Make a deliberate move to look only into their eyes and don't look away. Listen and watch carefully. Avoid the temptation of looking around for your next target, or some friend you promised to catch up with. That will all happen later. Stay in the moment with this one person. This is sometimes called making the other person feel they are the only person in the room and is simply a matter of focus. People will immediately like you a lot, largely because your focus on them is a form of flattery, affirming that their comments are important and that they are interesting.

Be precise, be brief

The longwinded person or the vague person generally fails at networking. Why? Because everything they do or don't do suggests that you are not important. Remember that perception is reality to others. So if they see you as not caring, they will believe this to be fact. That's why corporations and corporate leaders focus so strongly on perceptions.

In networking, the best perceptions are created by being precise and brief when you meet people. You may need to develop a brief standard opener before you go to a particular function or seminar. This should include who you are, what you do and what you're hoping to get out of the function or seminar. It could include an open-ended question for the other person, for example 'what did you get out of that last speech?'. This is far better than asking 'Did you like that last speech?' because that may only generate a 'Yes' or 'No' answer, and the conversation will stop. One corporate leader I know used to write down her proposed comments prior to a function or telephone conversation. This writing helped her to memorise them and lifted her confidence. Vague comments make you seem aloof and uncaring, so its best to avoid them—even if they are partly true. Comments like 'I'm only here because the boss said I should come' send the wrong messages.

Open up, lighten up

Being too serious about networking can make you less effective. After all, networking is just people getting to know people. It can help to open up about yourself; perhaps admitting a lack of understanding of some area or talking about a hobby that has nothing to do with work. Being ready to laugh and smiling a lot are encouraging signs for the other person, letting them know you are enjoying the chat. They are also signs that you will not be trying to sell them something. Many people attending functions are alert for the sales pitch and don't want to hear it, so keep it light and friendly.

> ... the best perceptions are created by being precise and brief ...

Set an agenda

The expression 'set the agenda' is just a corporate way of saying go to a function or meeting with a specific goal in mind. This goal may be to meet a particular person, communicate a single message or collect six business cards before you leave. Whatever the goal, the real benefit of setting an agenda for yourself is that it encourages you to talk and mix with new people. One successful journalist used to ask political leaders and corporate chiefs about their hobbies and turn the conversation to this specific interest. It had the benefit of putting these leaders at ease and adding a human dimension to the communication.

Introduce people

Once you become a little comfortable with networking, you will be more aware of opportunities to introduce people to others who share an interest. Most people react well to this because it shows you genuinely care about them. These introductions can be at any level. Perhaps you can introduce them to someone who needs their service or to someone who shares their passion for a particular sport. The subject doesn't matter so much; what matters here is that by introducing someone to another person, you have displayed a confidence in them and that you care about them. In other words, your communication takes a major leap forward.

Don't pin people down

Functions such as luncheons, seminars, conferences or after-work drinks are not occasions for the hard sell. If you believe networking equates to making a sale, think again. Networking is about making a contact, and ultimately making a friend. This will lead to sales, but later on. Never try to get an agreement or a commitment; that can come a few days later. Aggressive selling of your product, your service or yourself will become annoying to others. Networking involves a careful compromise between knowing that there is a long-term business purpose behind it and keeping it loose and social in the short term.

Always follow up

A few days after the event, send a note to everyone you met (that's why you'll need to collect those business cards). If you promised to find out something for a colleague, make the phone call and keep the promise. If you know that a person is looking for a business solution in a particular field, search through the media for an interesting article that you can copy and send to them. Keep the contact going; invite them to coffee or to lunch; treat the networking occasion as just the beginning. The more you stay in touch, the more certain you can be that you will remember their name, what they do and what their interests are.

> *Networking is about making a contact, and ultimately making a friend.*

7 NETWORK FOR SUCCESS

NETWORKING LESSONS FROM SCHOOLYARD BULLYING

A business leader learnt the importance of networking at school. He and his parents had moved to another town when he was eight years old, so he had to start at a new school. From the beginning at the new location, he had been harassed by schoolyard bullies. Picked on and isolated, his life had become miserable. In response, before he had even heard of the word 'networking', he set out to get to know lots of other kids. He joined in school plays and, although not sporty, even had a go at sports. This was an intuitive response that turned out to be inspired networking.

I would guess that part of his strength in adversity was that he actually liked himself and knew he had something to offer. Clearly he liked other people, because he wanted to get on with them, even if only for his own happiness. Plus he had lots of that core human drive for happiness. By being active and involved, he became known and cared for by many students. The bullying stopped. Perhaps it is part of the nature of bullies that they only pick on isolated people.

> *... if you don't have a network, you don't get ahead.*

What can this experience of bullying teach you about communication? In most businesses, especially in professional services (such as accountants and lawyers) or in trades (such as plumbing and building), if you don't have a network, you don't get ahead. Effective networks are groups of people who like each other and find each other useful. The simple truth behind networking is that people prefer to do business with people they know, like and trust.

THE IMPORTANCE OF NETWORKING

Elizabeth Foley is principal of a firm specialising in executive coaching, and she says of networking:

> *We have mixed feelings about it. Some people enjoy it, while others shy away. Some say they are not good at doing the 'small talk' thing, or just too busy. Others feel uncomfortable about networking because they see it as being shallow and for self-interest. Yet there are those who are very comfortable with it, who see it as a means to add satisfaction and value to their work and personal lives.*

She sees networking as a skill you can learn and points out that it is not really about small talk and insincerity. As she says: 'It is about being generous and genuine, by spending time with people, listening to them, and talking about what is really happening for us, sharing information about ourselves'. She advises people to approach networking with no expectations and see what they learn.

Her view is supported by Hugh Mackay, a social researcher. In his book *The Good Listener* (Macmillan Australia, 1994), Mackay says that people who feel insecure in relationships are unlikely to be good listeners. Networking is about building relationships, 'about making the channel of communication more open, more comfortable and more secure', Mackay says.

Foley adds that executives are more likely to be heard if they have built relationships through internal networking. Foley explains:

> *This doesn't necessarily mean having to go to the after-work drinks function. But it does mean face-to-face communication, having a cup of coffee together, making the phone call rather than sending an email, or stopping to chat for a few minutes in the corridor.*

... networking ... is not really about small talk and insincerity.

Careers and networking also go together, according to Foley. She states:

> *Networking can assist you achieve your career goals with your current employer. By having good relationships and open communication, an executive will feel more comfortable letting key people within the organisation know of their career aspirations or of their dissatisfaction in their current positions. The result could be a modification of the existing job, or a new position within the company.*

Joan Kirner and Moira Rayner are the authors of *The Women's Power Handbook* (Viking, 1999) and, with careers in politics and law, they clearly know what they're talking about. Their book is a great guide for both women and men and networking is a constant theme. As they say:

> *Networking is central to power, particularly woman-power. Personal networks really matter, whether you are in business, government, or politics, paid or unpaid. Write down all the networks you belong to. You'll be surprised how many you have: colleagues in the workplace; community groups; unions or professional organisations; local government councillors and staff; sporting contacts (yours, your partner's or your children's); your family, friends and neighbours; local businesses; ethnic or religious groups; students and schoolfriends; people you meet at pubs and clubs; the Internet; cultural groups; local childcare or kindergarten; lollipop ladies; and the people who run the local shop. You are well connected!*

Kirner and Rayner provide a powerful reminder that even if we don't think of ourselves as good networkers, we do actually have a pretty wide network already. We've made a good start, even before we think of networking.

They also provide a warning about networking: 'If you make connections with busy and influential people, the ones who can help you the most, don't ask for help or favours unless you're really serious'. That is, think before you act. If it is really important, then use your network as hard as you can, but don't waste your network on trivial things. A network is not a bottomless well, always ready to give what you want. There are limits, so use networks wisely.

Kirner and Rayner's summary on networking is worth noting:

> The key to networking is earning the right to ask a favour, or to be asked for a favour, and that comes from doing things for other people without always demanding something in return.

BUILDING A GROUP OF INFLUENTIAL FRIENDS

To build a network, start by writing down all the topics and activities you are interested in. Then select one or two that may be important for your personal life, career or business. Now plan ways to be involved in these. You could attend meetings of relevant groups or become a volunteer. This will help you to get to know as many people as possible. But be patient and accept that this can take time. Soon you will find you are being asked to do favours and can ask others to do favours for you. But be careful: networking requires subtlety, and it is not necessarily expected that you will blatantly ask for a quid pro quo.

> ... they have come to see a brand as a person with lots of networks.

BE YOURSELF

Marketers and advertisers are becoming more aware of the importance of personality in selling products, ideas or services. In a way, they have come to see a brand as a person with lots of networks. It can be helpful to use some of their thinking, even if it appears a little extreme. Consider, for example, how Kevin Roberts, CEO of global advertising agency Saatchi & Saatchi, described what he calls 'lovemarks' in a speech to the Ad-Tech Europe 2000 Conference in Amsterdam in October 2000. Roberts throws scorn on the conventional view of brand:

> Come up with a product. Trademark it. Give it a functional benefit. Write a marketing plan. Implement. The result? A great brand. Bullshit. Brands have smothered people with information. Now they're suffering the death

of a thousand yawns. A great brand has never had anything to do with all that stuff. A great brand has to be created with love, with inspiration, with emotion.

You can apply this brand thinking in your networking, for it is important to remember that you are a human being with passions, emotions and desires. Networking is a human activity, not a mechanical one. Just like developing a brand, networking involves humanisation. What will make you stand out as a networker is your personality. You don't have to be a great lawyer, a top sporting person or an accomplished musician—just network by being you. When you are networking, remember some of Roberts's advice: 'The adage about love holds true: to love others you first have to love yourself.' And to conclude his message:

> We all know that the greatest connections in life are built on love. This is how our partners, our friends and our families touch us. We all know that love links us in many different ways as couples who have been together for years, as parents and children, as close friends, as lovers. We all know that love needs time. I'm talking an investment of years. And we all know that love cannot be demanded. It can only be given. Take that knowledge you already have, and use it wisely.

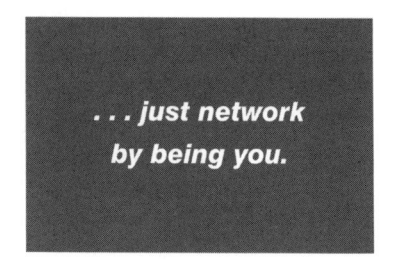

. . . just network by being you.

This, from the head of one of the most successful advertising agencies, advising some of the biggest global brands. If business can take heed of this message, surely you can too. Your networking will work better if it is fun, friendly, warm, shared, open, amusing, emotional and giving. You will succeed by being yourself, not by pretending to be an expert or something you are not. It is you, the person, that interests others most. So give a little.

SUPPORT A GOOD CAUSE

From corporate experience, getting behind a good cause is one of the best networking techniques of all. You benefit from being needed and from helping others. It's an effective way to build new relationships, become involved in the community, advance your own career or simply have fun. For people with a deep fear of communication or socialising, a good cause can be an important first step towards improved communication and a better self-image. Some of our best corporations support good causes, and find that they are happier places to be because of it.

This form of good corporate citizenship is often called 'cause-related marketing', otherwise known as sponsorship or community involvement. It links a company or brand to a relevant social cause or issue. It not only helps the cause, it also improves the company's or brand's consumer image. Companies choose causes that are related to their brand. Marketers call this 'relevance'. Cause-related marketing differs from straight donations because through it corporations aim to build their business. Surveys found that as many as 49 per cent of consumers would switch to a brand that supported a good cause of concern to them.

Cause-related marketing provides lessons for us all. If you want to get involved, choose a cause relevant to you personally or to your career. If, say, someone in your family has a disability, it would be logical to support a cause raising funds to assist research into that disability. If you work for a company with a major production plant in a small town, you could become involved in a fundraising or sporting group in that town. I know an accountant who joined a foundation raising funds for homeless children, a senior executive who supported an environmental research campaign, a solicitor who was the biggest supporter of a youth suicide prevention group and a plumber who raised funds within local Rotary. All enjoyed the experience, contributed greatly to these fine causes and helped their own careers in the process.

Some key advice on networking: if you are going to do it through a group or an activity, pick one that is of most natural interest to you, because you will be much more likely to stick with it.

If your involvement in a good cause is also helping you, it is likely that your contribution to the cause will be longer lasting and greater. This is not a totally selfish view; it just states the reality of how most of us can contribute the best. When there is also something in it for us, we will give more to it. Being involved in a good cause can help you build networks, gain a reputation for delivering results and receive personal benefits, such as happiness. If you've just moved to a new town or have more time on your hands, visit the library and read about community groups. Go along to the one that grabs your attention. Be open, go out and get involved. Your community needs you, and you need your community. If your company has just been taken over, find out which community groups or good causes the new company supports. Then find ways to help out. Doesn't this approach make networking seem like a very positive move? That's a recipe for good communication in a nutshell.

> When there is also something in it for us, we will give more to it.

PART 2

Using communication to rise to your potential

8 Influencing bosses and making friends   53
9 Creating real communication   61
10 From pitfalls to promotion   66
11 Promotion and persuasion   75
12 Leadership is already within you   84

INFLUENCING BOSSES AND MAKING FRIENDS

Wherever I meet people, I always have the feeling that I am encountering another human being, just like myself. I find it is much easier to communicate with others on that level. If we emphasise specific characteristics, like I am Tibetan or I am Buddhist, then there are differences. But those things are secondary. If we can leave the differences aside, I think we can easily communicate, exchange ideas and share experiences.
His Holiness, Tenzin Gyatso, the Fourteenth Dalai Lama

How do you break the ice and start talking with someone who has attracted you? This attraction may be in a business or purely personal context.

DON'T LET FEAR HOLD YOU BACK

Strangers can be interesting. Yet you may be fearful, or at least nervous, about making new friends. Bosses can control your future and your personal happiness. Again, you may have a fear of communicating with those above you. Fear of strangers and fear of leaders are common, and hold back many careers. I certainly had this fear in big quantities and time and time again it resulted in me not talking to the people who really mattered, at business and social functions. It could be a family function or a business reception, the same fear arose and I would find ways of dodging the people I knew I should talk to, or even wanted to talk to. When I tell colleagues of this fearful behaviour they are surprised because they have seen me working the room or networking among people I hardly know. But for me it was not always this way.

The lessons for making friends are there in corporate communication, for they have perfected the art of opening up new markets (just their way of saying they make new friends). The lessons hinge on the communication secret of combining mind and messages. By changing your attitudes plus learning a few skills, you can talk with virtually anyone.

The first step to influencing powerful people and making friends through effective communication is in your mind. A corporation would never start a new marketing campaign with a fearful attitude. Start with an open mind and you have already begun on the path to successful communication.

Many of us have a fear of elites and strangers, mostly arising from our chattering mind telling us that these people will not be interested or could be dangerous or we will run out of things to say. Most of us have this chattering mind at some level, and the key to success is to recognise it as just chatter, rather than following its confused fears. For example, many of us believe that the person we don't know or who is in charge is perfect and we are pathetically flawed, so they would never want to speak with us. This mental chatter is irrational and you can learn to note it, then ignore it. The 'note it, ignore it' technique for overcoming fear works because it can neutralise social fears. When the fear arises in your mind, note its presence. 'Ah, yes. Here's the old thought that no-one will like me' is all you need to think. Having noted it, the mind can move on, you can ignore it. Try it for yourself. If you do not note the negative thought, it will take control. Noting a thought is like exposing its weakness and putting you back in control.

We are also hindered by outdated views of what is acceptable communication. The combination of these two (your attitude and outdated standards) can leave you missing out on promotion, feeling lonely in a crowd, isolated at a party or one out in a team. It's awful and makes you miserable.

At the beginning of a communication training session for a partner in a legal firm, the partner told me that she felt uncomfortable in her core area of business—cultivating relationships with union officials. This lack of comfort and confidence was holding back her career. As she put it, 'I have nothing in common with them and I'm never going to be part of their group'. The first aspect of her problem was easy to address. If you genuinely like people, you will be astounded by how much we all have in common. For a start, we all have a desire for happiness. The second aspect of her problem was a feeling of insecurity that she could not communicate if she was not an accepted part of this union group. She came to recognise that this separateness was a strength because it made her more interesting and useful to the group. With this recognition, she was able to relax and communicate effectively.

> **If you genuinely like people, you will be astounded by how much we all have in common.**

Another approach is to look upon the fear as a positive energy. Good public speakers often have a feeling of fear prior to a speech, and see this as a positive way of putting them on their toes and ready to go. One speaker told me that before every speech she feels this intense knotting in the stomach, and every time it happens she recites in her mind: 'Welcome back, old friend, we're going to be on our toes out there'. She sees the knotting as a positive form of preparation, so she has transformed fear into a positive, simply by welcoming it.

If fear and anxiety have become a way of thinking for you, then their grip can be too strong and you will need to find assistance to overcome their control. Thinking about and visualising yourself in social situations will help—start by seeing yourself successfully chatting to one or two others. Gradually build the mental image, and practise. Don't try to become the life of the party overnight.

Fear of rejection can stop us making any move or asking any question. It is like a brick wall. Most of us take it personally if someone does not respond. Yet there could be hundreds of reasons for a person not responding, so why blame yourself? Also, don't try to be a mind-reader. It is a real barrier to communication. It is far better to assume that, at this stage, the person has a genuine reason for turning down your offer. Resolve to try again later instead of sulking off and reinforcing your attitudinal fears of starting a conversation.

Barry, a leading sales representative, told me he actually plans for rejection each week, expecting to be soundly turned down three times. None of the rejections hurt, because he expected them to happen. Note that he did not expect rejection all the time (otherwise it could become a self-fulfilling prophecy) but only three times out of about fifty contacts each week. In his mind, this was not bad. The result was that none of the rejections dented his confidence.

REACHING OUT TO THE PEOPLE YOU NEED

When we do things with other people (become active, join in or start a project) we create friends. The ways to make new friends can be learned from our best corporations, many of whom have perfected the art.

One of the greats of corporate PR, Edward Bernays, created a campaign for Proctor & Gamble in 1923 for Ivory soap and the reasoning behind it holds true today. Children were the targets of the campaign. Far from being the 'friends' of soap, most kids saw soap as the enemy. How could he encourage children to make friends with soap? The first thing Bernays did was to listen to people, via a survey. The results showed a preference for white unperfumed soap over others. Since Ivory was the only white un-perfumed soap on the market, he emphasised this to the media and the word was out. He used events to add interest and to get people involved, rather than just listening. For a quarter of a century, the National Soap Sculpture Competition in White Soap got millions of kids actively involved with the product, conditioned to enjoy using Ivory. By appealing to their sense of creativity and fun, soap became their friend not their enemy.

The communication lessons here for you, as you seek new friendships, are:

- Listen to people.
- Speak their language.
- Don't be scared of being different.
- Create something interesting to do.
- Make relationships a bit of fun.

These are the things Bernays did so successfully for Proctor & Gamble.

Creative interaction comes up repeatedly in successful corporate PR. The PR consultancy Spector and Associates Inc. had the task of making AT&T the leading Internet access provider. They needed more than mere publicity. They turned to interaction, as is laid out on their fascinating website, www.prmuseum.com. To quote from the site:

> *We created a series of informative and interactive web pages: the Genealogy page, Back-To-School page, Golf page and People Finder page. These showed people how to use the Internet to enhance their lives, explore personal interests, trace their family history, find old friends, and gave them the confidence to delve further and unleash its vast potential.*

What a great reminder this campaign is about how to build friendships. If you have no action, you will have no friends. Most of us believe that actions speak louder than words, reinforcing that interaction and friendship go together. You don't build friends if you stay at home, avoid the phone or stay away from public gatherings.

> *If you have no action, you will have no friends.*

Once you've broken the ice, two points will help you develop better personal and business communication: first, convince yourself to really like everyone you meet; second, make sure that in every conversation you ask the other person some questions.

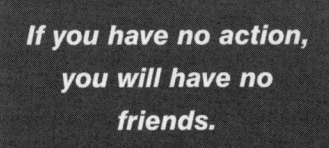

USING POSITIVE BODY LANGUAGE

Corporations know that how they look reflects on how they are perceived by people. That's why they spend so much on presentation, such as decor and design. It's their form of corporate body language. Your body language will either help or hinder you in making new friends. If fear dominates your brain, it will also rule your body. For example, an indirect gaze instead of maintaining eye contact is seen by others as evasive, ear-pulling indicates doubt, slumped shoulders show lack of confidence and turning your body away signifies rejection of what the other person is saying. On the other hand, a good impression is created by eye contact. It is improved with a smile, showing friendly attention.

First impressions are important, so it is worth giving your attention to the detail of your own body language. There are body language experts who can help you with making friends. Here are the best tips that I have put to work for my corporate clients.

- **Move forward.** To make friendly contact, physically move towards the other person. At a social function, that may mean standing inside their group, then moving closer to begin a personal conversation.
- **Lean forward.** When starting to talk to a stranger, lean forward to show that you are interested. Leaning back tells them you do not care, are too tired or not interested.
- **Have an open stance.** If your arms and legs are crossed, it tells the other person you are defensive and protective, unwilling to listen and very scared.
- **Make eye contact.** Eye contact is the key to personal communication success. Throw caution to the wind and focus on their eyes. If your mind is saying you like people and they like you, close eye contact will be easier.
- **Be responsive.** When the other person talks, you will encourage more conversation if you nod, raise your eyebrows or show some other reaction.
- **Smile.** Leaving the most important to last—in creating new friendships, start with a smile. Everyone understands a smile. It says you are open, comfortable and happy, which is a great combination for most people.

BE HAPPY

David Ogilvy, founder of global advertising agency Ogilvy & Mather, was one of the giants of the advertising industry last century. One of his themes was 'Be happy while you are living', and he identified this happiness as a key to effective communication and making new friends. In his book, *Ogilvy on Advertising* (Pan Books, 1983), he said:

> *Most of the people I know in agencies strike me as well cast for their work and reasonably happy in it. Whenever I think that someone is wasting his talents in advertising, I tell him so. One of my partners is a superb naturalist, and secretly resented every day he spent in the agency. On my advice he retired—and went on to save endangered species of fauna from extinction. In the words of the Scottish proverb, 'Be happy while you're living, for you're a long time dead'.*

This is a great tip for influencing powerful people and making new friends: if you are happy with yourself, people will feel it and be attracted to you. If you are unhappy, others will know. We do not flock to unhappy people.

UNDERSTANDING PERSONALITY TYPES

Most of us hate to categorise people, but for corporate PR this form of analysis is essential. Corporations spend a lot of money analysing the target audience, getting to know them before the company starts to talk or sell to them. Knowledge first; communication second. This sequence could work for you in seeking promotion and creating friendships. It is a matter of following the corporate lead and thinking first of your boss or friend rather than of yourself. If you put an understanding of the other person first, you will communicate on their terms and be more easily understood. Thinking of others is the best way to look after yourself. Don't put people in tight boxes, but do realise that we all have differences and you will make better friends if you are aware of these differences.

Most audience categorisation systems are too complex to use in making friends. For example, the marketing and PR industries have long used the Myers-Briggs type indicators, dividing people into sixteen personality types. This is just not practical for everyday life. One of the easiest forms of categorisation I have seen is called 'brainstyles', created by Marlane Miller (*Brainstyles: Change Your Life Without Changing Who You Are*, Simon & Schuster, 1997). Many PR consultants have used Miller's system with their corporate clients. My own clients have benefited from it, for both external and internal staff communication. Miller created four distinct personality types or brainstyles. These are discussed below. Think about your boss, friends, potential friends and work colleagues in these ways; once you know these characteristics, you can tailor your communication messages better.

> *Thinking of others is the best way to look after yourself.*

The knower

This person is logical and quick to analyse—a real problem solver. Their left brain dominates. However, they can seem cold and unemotional, or highly competitive and intolerant of plodders.

The conciliator

Dominated more by the right brain, these people are just about the opposite of the knowers. Conciliators live in the moment and respond emotionally. They are creative, responsive and inventive. Seen as gifted in interpersonal relationships, they are natural networkers. On the other hand, they can lose motivation and need to be kept on the task. Without recognition, they quickly drop a project. People we call 'high maintenance' are conciliators. We all know someone like this.

The conceptor

These people use both sides of the brain well and produce original and powerful communication. They march to a different drum, and don't mind being seen that way. They can easily turn the course of a meeting or discussion. They are risk takers and can drive pretty hard for their own ideas, making them individualistic and difficult. They sometimes have trouble getting the message across to us mere mortals, and accordingly become frustrated and agitated. You will always be in for some surprises from friends like this, so keep your mind alert and open.

The deliberator

The most balanced of the four types, their strength is analysis, planning and rational responses, but it could all take a long time. This is not a concern for the deliberator but can drive others crazy. Once they have worked out a solution, they often achieve consensus for it and then stick to it single-mindedly.

They say you really know people when you see them under pressure or in a crisis. To sum up the four different types of people, this is how each would react in time of crisis:

- **The knower** will think for a second, then propose a rational solution, confidently, right then and there.
- **The conciliator** will respond emotionally, shooting off a series of highly charged and creative solutions.
- **The conceptor** will quickly invent a theory to cover all the facts, feeling comfortable that they have put the crisis in context.
- **The deliberator** will take the crisis apart, analyse it and build a rational solution. But this will take some time.

So, there you have it: the four main types of personality. Overriding these, all human beings have one important thing in common: we all want to be happy. Even the boss who turned down your last request for promotion has the basic desire for personal happiness. This common desire outweighs any differences, but understanding differences can help us understand each other better. Applying these types to bosses, friends and colleagues can mean you become better at getting your message across. If you are still a little squeamish about being so structured as to categorise people, consider that it is surely better to think of others before thinking of yourself. Categorisation merely improves your ability to think of others. Once you know who they are, you can stop trying to change them or communicate with them in ways

> *...understanding differences can help us understand each other better.*

that simply do not work well for their type. It works in corporate communication and can make you a better communicator. A good starting point is to use these brainstyles for self-analysis. Which type are you?

Don't get bogged down on categorisation. Instead, use it as a tool to gain a quicker understanding of people and to reduce your fears. From there, implement these three tips for influencing powerful people and building new friendships: be yourself; live in the present; and like other people.

CREATING REAL COMMUNICATION 9

DON'T TAKE PEOPLE FOR GRANTED

I hate those corporate videos where a booming, deep male voice is talking *at* me. Why do corporations choose voice-over people who could be army sergeants? 'Pay attention! Listen up! Wash your hands!' These heavy voice-over techniques are not good communication; they are a mistake. They are left over from an old view of communication: that we are the targets and all you have to do is load the message into the arrow and fire it at the target. Surely, the old marketers thought, this would get the message across. Corporate study has shown this view to be wrong. It's great that we don't fall for this. We are not passive targets; we are individuals with reactions and visions of our own. So when you deliver a message to us, it needs to fit with those reactions and visions. For most of us, that means shouting messages at us will not work because it will not get the message across. This is true in the business world and in your personal life. When thinking about your friendships, you can learn from these corporate mistakes. Not that deep booming voices are the problem, but rather you can learn from what is implied when people talk at other people.

There is a radical change in the way companies are dealing with their customers, caused partly by the Internet and partly by a realisation that the old ways were faulty. Most of their marketing involved talking *at* us, rather than *with* us. Even worse, these companies only ever talked when they wanted to sell. Outside the sale, they showed no interest in us. How dangerous this is in personal life.

> ... these companies only ever talked when they wanted to sell.

One of my friends is always happy to have a chat on the phone, but never calls me. He always enjoys meeting for a drink, but he never organises it. He'll come along to a sporting event, but only if asked. Worse, he'll part company with a cheery 'I'll call you during the week', but always forgets to. On the few occasions he has made a call, it has been for a specific reason, not just to have a chat. We're still mates because I think it is worth the effort, but what if my life became too busy or changed in some way? It's a fair guess that our friendship would fall aside.

Mass marketing and mass messages, once the heroes of marketing, have been largely discredited. Today, companies are trying to treat each customer as an individual. They know that what they call a 'market' does not work by one side (the company) just loading arrows (messages) and firing them at the other side (customers) with the hope that a few will hit the mark. Now the proposition is put that these markets are places for conversations between human beings.

This thinking can work in your friendships, because it will help you avoid placing your friends into categories or boxes, not allowing for their growth and diversity. Confined friendships, where you place someone in a box, become stifling and either go nowhere or disappear. Have you seen those married couples who keep each other firmly in a box? 'He never likes cakes' is said more as an order or accusation than a comment. 'She couldn't care about sports' is a prelude to some complaint. 'He only goes to action movies' is the excuse for never challenging his comfort zone and taking him to the latest tear-jerker. I think the comfort zone in many couples is self-imposed, designed to restrict rather than enhance, to prevent change rather than encourage growth. Customers treated in this way generally go away after a while so, if this applies to your relationships, be wary.

Companies are accepting that markets today are smarter and can communicate in many ways. This is posing a real problem for old-fashioned retailers who want to treat us as numbers. 'No, thanks', is our response.

Most people do not want to hear a corporate sales pitch. We can now turn these sales pitches off. We are not stuck, having to listen. It's good to think of your personal friends in this way too. They do not have to listen to you, meet with you or respond in any way at all. They do not want to hear your prepared speeches; they want to get close to the real you. And they want you to get close to the real them. So if you approach your friends with more of an open mind, feeling pleasure in their company, you can then start some real dialogue, which in turn develops the friendship.

> **Behind the thinking is the view that 'We are all in this together'.**

'Partnership' has been one of the business buzzwords of the corporate world, referring to a change wherein companies treat their suppliers and other businesses as partners. More than just a word change, this has heralded a new era of cooperative thinking, joint problem solving and better business-to-business relationships. Behind the thinking is the view that 'We are all in this together'. This can be a good starting point for your close relationships too. Accept that your own happiness and the happiness of others are interdependent, and you will have made a big step forward in relationships.

Saatchi & Saatchi is one of the world's advertising and ideas powerhouses, and some of the best thinking about marketing and communication comes from their leadership. Sandra Yates, Chairperson of their Australian firm, has called for marketers to 'reinvent conversations'. Her view is that business has to stop talking *at* people. Yates tells their corporate clients that for a brand to succeed it must be trusted by people, and trust is something that has to be earned, over time. Surely it is just the same for friendships; they build trust over time, and fail when trust has failed.

In business, Yates has identified what she calls a 'conversation revolution' where people are talking to each other and 'transforming the language of business'. What does this change mean for business? Yates says:

> *The great challenge for all of us in business is to understand that if we want to grow our businesses, develop our brands, and add value for our shareholders, then we have to engage all our shareholder groups in conversation. We must stop telling, and start asking. We must stop answering questions nobody asked, and try to figure out the real questions people want us to respond to. We need to develop our listening skills, and every communication should be in the language of our customers, not the language of business.*

This hits a powerful point for all of us as we build friendships and careers. It's not just a business message, though I wonder how many businesses could meet her demands?

Having recently done a run through some corporate websites, I'm depressed about the failure of many businesses to achieve real conversations. While the Web is modern communication, the language many companies use on the Web is the same old business jargon that didn't work in the older formats. It does not work on the Web, because it is either paternalistic or boring, or both.

Just as the communication effectiveness of corporations fluctuates, so too you should not expect always to be perfect, always to make and keep friends and to have life on a totally even plane. Life's not even. Life changes, and so do you. This makes it even more important never to take bosses, colleagues or friends for granted. Work hard at keeping and building relationships. We never seem to achieve a level performance, and while this makes life interesting and dynamic, it also means that those who want to improve need to know where they are in communication at any given time.

By doing a communication 'balance sheet' of where you are falling down and where you are

> **Life's not even. Life changes, and so do you.**

doing well, it may become clear to you why you missed out on that promotion or why you currently have lots of social engagements. It could reveal why the boss overlooked you for that special project, why you feel stuck in a rut, why your relationships have soured or even why you are making new friends with greater ease. By accepting that you will never operate in an even way, you can come to understand the fluctuations and work to change them. By doing a balance sheet you may see quite clearly why your best friend is not calling and, more importantly, you can take action to renew the friendship. Without a balance sheet you may never know where you are or why things are going wrong.

As companies strive to deal with us as people, instead of market segments, they provide lessons that can improve your communication:

- Don't take anyone or anything for granted.
- Be open to changes as people change.
- Listen a lot.
- Don't speak *at*, have a discussion *with*.
- Accept that 'We are all in this together'.

NETWORKING IN NEW SITUATIONS

What about communicating in new work locations, during takeovers and with new bosses and colleagues? What can we learn from corporations, many of which are expert at opening new markets (making new friends)?

Friends and contacts support us every day. As we go about our work, in our community or in our homes, friends provide one key to success: we are social animals. When you move to a new location, or find yourself in the middle of a corporate merger or takeover, making friends and new contacts is a real issue. How do you make new friends? How do you have a positive impact on new bosses? You will have less chance of building a good social group if your mind is driven by fear, especially fear of failure. It is time to put fears to the back of your mind and focus on good communication. Remember that fear is the road to failure; communication is the highway to success.

Corporations, too, have to make new 'friends' from time to time, and you can learn from their experience. For example, if a company is opening a new plant in a new location, it makes local friends. If a company is about to introduce itself to a new market, it first sets out to make friends. How do corporations make new friends?

- **They get out and meet people.** Corporations accept that if they stay in their office castles they will soon become isolated and friendless. They spend a lot of money to make sure their people can get out there and mix with people. If you shut the front door and watch

TV, you will never meet people and make friends. It can be hard, but the benefits of getting out of your home and into the community are too great to miss.
- **They become involved in the local community.** For some corporations, this may be as simple as sponsoring local sporting clubs. Becoming involved is a valuable lesson as you strive for more friendships. Join a club, play a sport, go to church, take an evening class or become a volunteer. The more you are involved, the more you will meet people and that is the beginning of friendship.

One of the best corporate networkers had some key lessons he liked to pass on to the younger people in his team. Training them to network, to get to know people and become more important to the people they met, his key messages were:

- Like people and consider each person as potentially important to you.
- Accept social chitchat, no matter how superficial.
- Operate on various levels, depending on the other person's interest.
- Get out of your comfort zone, if that's what it takes to make a connection.
- Ask people about an aspect of themselves as a starter (most people love to talk about themselves).
- Accept that some relationships will never work, and simply move on from failure.

Bruce, a partner in a leading accounting firm, has a golden rule for his after-hours networking. He only accepts invitations for events or joins boards or committees for things that really interest him. He figures that if he is interested in the activity, he will be happy to be there, and being happy will be communicated to others and make him more interesting. It's like a happiness and interest circle. You can apply this in your private life. Don't take up a craft because someone thought it would be good for you when what you really wanted was to play darts in the local team. If you are doing what you want to do, friendships will follow.

But you will also need to be patient. Friendship takes time; promotion may not happen overnight. As Aristotle said, 'Friendship is slow ripening fruit'. Don't rush it. You will get there, provided you get out and have a go.

10 FROM PITFALLS TO PROMOTION

LISTEN, THINK AND DO

I have often described communication within the corporate environment as a process involving two or three steps. In the two-step process, we think and then we do. Much better is the three-step process, where we listen, think and then do. These three steps can take a long time for a corporation, involving market research, analysis and planning prior to getting on with the job. As individuals, each step can occur virtually simultaneously and instantly, but the three steps do occur.

We all know people who suffer from 'talk before they think' syndrome. They are probably doing both steps, but getting a bit jumbled in the process so that the 'do' happens before they are ready. Remember that here we are discussing a process that takes less than a second in our mind. Effective communicators get the right balance and timing between the two steps of think and do.

People who fail to get the message across rarely use the sequence of listen, think and do. They just stumble around, expecting to fail. Possibly, most people are not even aware that there are the two steps of think and do or the three of listen, think and do.

Some corporations miss the proper sequence too, and their communication fails as a result. For example, a corporation can become so focused on market research and finetuning their understanding of what people think, that they never actually convey their corporate messages. Others are too hasty, starting communication programs before they really know enough about what the market is thinking. You can learn from these corporate mistakes. Does this happen to you? Do you ever become so preoccupied with what others are thinking that you fail to send out your own messages? Or do you shoot off the message too soon, before you even have a clue whether it is the right one, for the right person, at the right moment?

My theory is that when people feel a failure, their communication stops at the first step of thinking and rarely gets to the second step of doing. Feelings of failure create a blockage. This is how we can tell that something is wrong with that friend or colleague. Failure creates silence. When people feel that they have failed, their focus becomes negative and internal, so that often they will think about a communication but never do it. Instead, it happens in their mind.

For anyone with clients, this failure syndrome is more obvious. Clients do not want silence. They look for affirmation, reinforcement and some creative input from their consultant, whether it is in a sales role or in providing a professional service, such as legal, accounting, engineering or architecture. Clients find silence disturbing. In this way, feelings of failure breed actual failure. A disturbed client will look elsewhere. This may not be at once, because perhaps they have received good service and advice, but eventually they will move on from the consultant who is stuck on the think stage of communication, never providing the do stage that is so vital for genuine two-way communication.

A psychotherapist friend agrees with my theory, and related to me the following case study. The wife of one 'failure' could sit with him in the same room night after night but feel that he was closed off and that communication was not welcome. Often, she would say things he did not hear and therefore did not respond to. No doubt his hearing did pick up the sound of her voice, but something stopped his brain from registering the message. 'Did you say something?' was a phrase he frequently used, while she said 'Did you hear me?' or 'You never listen to what I say' just as often. He would be surprised that they had a social engagement and claim that he had not been told. There were details about the progress of their children that he had been told, but not actually heard. When her comment did register, his response was limited because his brain was really off somewhere else and did not want to come back to this time. Compounding the issue was that he would think responses, but not say them. Sometimes, he would actually be convinced that he had said them, but find out later that he had remained silent. This was a surprise to him.

> ... feelings of failure breed actual failure.

This is a bleak and frightening picture, going way beyond my field of communication. If you can relate to even one part of this, consider talking to an expert, such as a therapist or counsellor. Help is available. In the end, you cannot keep a sense of failure to yourself. Others will know about it, but have no idea how to help. That's where professionals, such as therapists and counsellors, come in. After you have straightened out the internal problem, you can get back into real communication and move on from failure. The first step is to acknowledge the powerful blockage between thinking and doing, and how dangerous this blockage is to relationships.

> In the end, you cannot keep a sense of failure to yourself.

DODGING MIRAGES

Many of us have created mirages in our minds about what successful communication is. More exactly, we have firm views on why some people are great communicators and, generally, why we are so hopeless. Each element of these mirages can be exposed, helping you get on with the important task of communicating your way to greater happiness.

Mirage number one

This mirage involves telling ourselves that communication is for the stars. 'That person is a born communicator', we tell ourselves. Meanwhile, we tell ourselves that we are not stars. This is negative and false. Everyone can communicate. Everyone can use communication to improve interpersonal relationships. Most of the people we admire as good communicators have actually been through some form of training. The reality is that good communicators are made, not born. If they have learned the art of communication, why can't you?

Mirage number two

Here we think that communication is all about instant results, and since our own communication does not give us the power to get what we want, it must have failed. In reality, all communication produces results. Something will happen when we communicate. What is important is how you communicate, how you behave, how positive your thoughts are and so on. Also remember that the greatest results from communication are the 'intangibles' such as friendship, respect, intimacy and involvement. Perhaps you need to put more value on these intangibles.

> ... the greatest results from communication are the 'intangibles' ...

Mirage number three

This mirage leads us to believe that any new communication approach is better than the old one. To move from a failure to a success, according to this mirage, we need a totally new communication approach. This view promotes the idea of 'out with the old, in with the new'. In this ruthless quest for success, we can erode friendships, reduce trust and create an atmosphere of tension and competition. It is not good communication, nor is it clear thinking, to believe that you will only get your message across if you change totally. Improved communication is a gradual process. As such, it can help you in gradual growth and gradual change, but it is not a matter of throwing out the old and bringing in the new. Take one step at a time on the path to better

> Improved communication is a gradual process.

communication. Let improvements cascade out, rather than storm through the door. As you improve, and as your relationships build better understanding, move on to a new level of communication.

Mirage number four

Here we believe that to communicate well we must conform. This is the yes-man syndrome. We know that corporations where people are just clones do not go too far, and it is the same at a personal level. Be yourself. Differences are exciting and they make us strong as groups. Learn communication skills so that you are listened to and taken seriously, but don't conform in the mistaken view that this will help. It will not, because people can often see through to the real you anyway.

THE 'HAPPINESS PRINCIPLE'

A client, who was a leading accountant, needed help understanding how PR skills could help his younger accountants succeed. Struggling for the simplest way to express it, I found myself saying, 'PR is about putting your best foot forward'. It has turned out to be the most simple and effective description of PR that I have ever created. I went on to tell him that our most successful corporations always put their best foot forward. They build their communications on being good and happy places to work and delivering on their promises. Look how many advertisements these days show organisations as fun places to be. Another way of saying they put their best foot forward is to say they put on a happy face. Ten years ago my corporate colleagues would have laughed if I had said that, but today most of them are also building communication around the 'happiness principle'. As a communication consultant to many corporations, I have never told a client to put their worst foot forward, nor, importantly, have I told them to lie. A good rule of thumb is give 'em your best, but make sure it's the truth.

> **They build their communications on being good and happy places to work...**

To communicate better, improve relationships, overcome fear of others, build personal happiness and advance your career, here are eight tips (call them the 'happiness principle') drawn from my corporate experience.

Care about people

Corporations call this market research. I call it caring about people. If you care, you will want to know what they think and how they feel. Successful corporations identify their market, and then they set out to make this market happy. Once the corporation knows what these important people think (especially about their product, their competitors and the general environment in which they operate), they can tailor their messages to work best. Hence, Coca-Cola communicates about fun and desirable people, rather than how they make the stuff. On the other hand, Mack trucks tell their audience (cynical and tough fleet buyers) exactly how the machines are made, rather than how much fun you can have in a Mack. See the difference?

Create a real conversation

It is not just what you say that counts. What really counts is how the conversation goes. Good corporations value conversations, because they value responses from the people that matter to them. They ask: how was our communication received? What feedback did we get? To get the answers, good corporations know they need to create a conversation, which means becoming better at listening and asking questions. Good communicators ask lots of questions. Asking questions is an almost foolproof way of keeping a conversation going.

Continue by rejecting the silly notion that, 'I said it, therefore you understand it'. I hear chief executives complaining that they've spent a fortune advertising a message and still nobody knows it. Many instances of communication breakdown occur because one side believes it has said it, while the other side claims it never heard it. Through feedback (listening to others and asking questions) you find out if people have received your message. Without feedback you are only guessing that the message got across. 'Why don't they understand?' This line is heard in most domestic arguments. As one of the best spin doctors once said: 'You might say "boo" to a goose, but what does the goose hear?'.

Don't give up—talk some more

Good corporate communication is not instant, nor is it easy. It succeeds through long-term, painstaking repetition of credible messages. I advise my corporate clients that when they are totally bored with a corporate message, it might be just starting to get through to their target audience. It's much the same for people. So, stick to the communication task is the lesson—phone a friend now. On the other hand, notice how your colleagues and friends fall away if you forget to make contact? You will be more likely to persevere if you make sure you like the people you live, work and deal with.

Be truthful

The best corporate PR programs have honesty as a core policy. Cynics may suggest it is fear of being caught out, more than a real commitment, that makes them honest. In a way, it hardly matters why. For good corporations, honesty is a central part of their happiness culture. In your life and career, it is best to follow this corporate lead and be known for accuracy and sticking to the facts. The flip side is never cover up a weakness or a mistake. You get found out.

Admit mistakes

Corporations have learnt from bitter experience that when people find out something too late, they are angry and do not seek to understand their point of view. That's why the best corporations will be up front and honest about mistakes, acknowledging the error and committing to finding better ways to do business in future. As you build relationships or climb the career ladder, make sure you have a reputation for disclosing problems, rather than for covering them up. You will make mistakes. Covering up holds you back; acknowledging mistakes allows you to move on.

Be interesting

In the corporate world, we in PR say that being interesting is a matter of tailoring the message to the specific interests of various target audiences. Tailor your message to whomever you are talking to, otherwise it becomes boring or mumbo jumbo. Don't talk football at length to someone whose passion is opera. Note also that good corporate communicators add some humour or fun to their messages. If you must talk football to your opera-loving friend, start by asking them, 'Why do you think I love football so much?'. You will get some interesting answers, plus you have started a dialogue that includes your favourite topic. Always make sure you are having a bit of fun, even in the serious side of business.

Be specific

The best organisational messages relate to a specific new initiative, new product, change in approach, improved earnings or other action. If you are specific and action-oriented, your relationships and career really take off.

Stick to the facts

Organisations making bold claims they cannot support are quickly carved up by the media and criticised by analysts. So, when promoting yourself, avoid exaggeration. A common corporate communication mistake is to make too many promises or to claim too much. Those who are a bit shy, on the other hand, have the reverse problem. Most of us communicate in a way that puts ourselves down. There is a middle road. Remember, you are actually better than you may think you are.

A parent confided in me that her teenage daughter had fallen into a pattern of exaggerating everything, so far that she could barely distinguish between what she said and the truth. The corporate messages of stick to the facts and always tell the truth were not much use to this girl, because the exaggeration had become a habit. Fortunately, the parent had discussed this with her daughter. The girl said that she knew her exaggeration was an attempt to impress, but she could not control it: 'It just comes out that way'. Most of us have done this from time to time.

She did it all the time, and so it was a major personal and communication problem.

Drawing clear professional boundaries, I advised the mother that low self-esteem was probably playing a part in making the girl want to impress others, and that the key to understanding this could be found through counselling or some other form of mind awareness. I also suggested a technique I have used for executives who have trouble engaging in social chitchat. I call the technique 'celebrate the mundane'. This is based on the reality that we certainly admire people who demonstrate knowledge and insight, but we also appreciate those who merely open up and be natural. This starts with what we normally see as the mundane aspects of our lives. Try telling people about your experiences in going to the shop, or report what you did before work. People are interested in how the bus trip went, preparing for sport, forgetting to bring your lunch, what you chose to watch on TV and the 'Did you see?' questions that can relate to that day's newspapers or last night's TV. Too many of us see these as mundane and we stick to more professional or, in the teenage daughter's case, more glamorous and exciting information. As you report these mundane events of life, do so as if they are ordinary and low key. The results are generally amazing, because conversation flows and a feeling of goodwill is generated. The mother determined to pass this on to her daughter, as part of the solution to habitual exaggeration.

The daughter found that after talking with friends about the mundane, she felt happier, because exaggerating left her feeling unsatisfactory. She found it hard to stick to, but perseverance is needed in all aspects of effective communication.

SPEAK + LISTEN + REPEAT

You can learn from successful corporations, many of which base their communication on three steps: speak + listen + repeat = success in communication.

Speak, but keep it simple

Good corporations know that to communicate about themselves and their products, they need to agree on a set of simple themes that collectively sum them up. Even the most sophisticated organisations learn to speak simply. Some spend a fortune on creative talent and copywriters to create six or ten phrases that tell the corporate story. The idea is that everybody from the top down is then supposed to use those phrases, so the message cascades out to the target audience. Establishing and agreeing on some central statements about the corporation is an important step in corporate communications. These are invariably very simple phrases.

For you, this means think before you talk. In this way, you will be developing simple themes that ensure your communication works for you. Let me give you a simple example. If, out of the blue, someone asks you 'How are things?' you may give a mumbled response, which is pretty unsatisfying to the other person. Something like 'Not too bad' is a poor answer, communicating uncertainty about yourself. But if you have a ready-made summary (such as 'This has been one of the busiest times for me at work, but fortunately the kids have settled in beautifully at school and everything is going well') you can leave the listener feeling positive about you. Don't overdo this, because that can be as bad as the mumbled response.

Listen to me

Modern corporations spend a small fortune finding out what people, especially their customers, think. Listening is a skill you can learn. By asking questions, as well as being quiet when your brain screams that you want to make a point, you will get on better with people. The best listeners are generally the best communicators. They become good listeners by maintaining eye contact. They look closely at the speaker, treating their words with close attention and respect. They are not diverted from conversations by people's movement. Good listeners often sum up what the other person said, but in their own words, just to check that they got the message. Often they will say, with enthusiasm, 'So your point here is that . . .' Good listeners do not get frightened by a short time of silence. They know that after silence, the other person may offer more information. They use silence to draw the other person out.

> **The best listeners are generally the best communicators.**

Tell me again

Human beings have a great capacity to forget. That's why we communication consultants, so-called 'spin doctors', can make a living. To get on with people or to get ahead you will almost certainly have to repeat your key messages. Like corporations, say the same things in new and entertaining ways.

Many people go through life complaining that they cannot get what they want. In their experience, communication rarely advances their cause. It's sad if people leave it at that, accepting communication failure. Communication can be a way towards your goals, contributing to your success as a person and in your career. You don't need the gift of the gab or to attend a long course to get the qualifications to communicate. The skills can be learned. A simple yet structured approach to communication (speak + listen + repeat) could mean you do get what you want.

Translating my corporate experience to the individual, I would advise that a combination of liking people, including yourself, and being truthful and inquisitive will make you a good communicator and a successful follower of the 'happiness principle'.

PROMOTION AND PERSUASION

HOW TO GET PROMOTED

Sooner or later, most of us ask ourselves: where do I go from here? You may be stuck in a rut, looking for a job or wondering why you have missed out on promotion. Do you have the courage and confidence to chase promotion or change? If so, do you have the art of persuasion, to get what you want? If promotions or opportunities are passing you by, you may waste time looking for others to blame for your circumstances. Yet the chances are you need look no further than yourself. Why is this so? Poor communication and a fear of others are the most common causes of failure. They stop us becoming the person we could be. Other people always seem to be confident, and part of you is not surprised they get promoted first. But, deep down, you know promotion should be yours. Improving your communication skills (and therefore reducing fear) will help you gain promotion.

> *Poor communication and a fear of others are the most common causes of failure.*

Many corporate chief executives are blind to real talent and get the people side of their business wrong. They either promote the wrong people or miss out on a lot of good people because they just don't notice them. These bosses believe that if you're good, there is no need for self-promotion because you'll be noticed and get the better job. This view is partly right. Yes, generally, good people stand out because they are often effective communicators, with self-promotion coming almost naturally. But it is also partly wrong: what about good people who are less effective at self-promotion?

You can improve your chances of a new job or a promotion by listening to some of the things chief executives have told me about the subject.

One, leading a major investment company, says he looks for three qualities in people: imagination, flexibility and loyalty. This is a good guide. People with ideas do attract leaders, and it is important to combine ideas and communication. Flexibility impresses most employers because they know that things can change. If you

> *Flexibility impresses most employers because they know that things can change.*

75

can review what you are doing and change when needed, you will attract attention. The third quality—loyalty—raises the point that the competition is not inside the organisation, it's outside. It is best to avoid the unpleasant politics that goes with many larger organisations.

Another client, who was managing partner of a professional services firm, looked for five qualities in any future partner within the practice: enthusiasm, communication, care, enjoyment and performance. Enthusiasm compensates for lack of long-term experience, according to him. Communication was critical to his firm because it is a service provider, so all partners needed to be able to relate to clients. As one lawyer said, 'There is no point in knowing the answers and not being able to implement them—and that requires communication'. Care comes from empathy with clients. Enjoyment, on the other hand, comes from striking a balance between work and private life. The final point of performance is that if you are really good at what you do, you have the beginnings of being your own best advertisement.

Good people may stand out like beacons, but for every good person who stands out, there could be as many as two or three unrecognised and unrewarded, purely because they cannot communicate. This may not be fair, but it does demonstrate that at work the crucial thing is to get noticed.

My own list of pointers to help in promotion is:

- Be enthusiastic.
- Don't be afraid to try new ideas.
- Move on from any small failures.
- Talk a lot, laugh a little.
- Share your dreams.

I could add 'smile and be happy', but you probably will anyway if you follow this list. As you follow the new course of action, you may find that the old fear comes back. Expect it to come back and, when it does, recognise it and have confidence your new communication skills will allow you to overcome it.

MASTERING THE ART OF PERSUASION

If you are going to move upwards and achieve more, you will need to pick up the skills to master the art of persuasion. A common mistake is that people link persuasion with hard sell. The problem with coming on with the hard sell is that it gives others something to disagree with or fight against, and so it can invite opposition rather than agreement. Persuasion is also a matter of give and take. You need to be prepared to compromise. It shows that you are open to the concerns of others and are flexible. It is also a mistake to confuse argument with persuasion. You may argue your position beautifully, but it is only part of the story and you need also to create empathy with others, connect with them and create some emotion. Persuasion is also rarely a one-shot effort. Like so many parts of communication, you need to be prepared to try, try again. Persuasion can be slow and difficult, but it is worth the effort. It helps you move forward and upward. The art of persuasion has five main elements.

Connect emotionally

Emotion works two ways in persuasion. First, we need to show our commitment to whatever we are advocating, whether it be career advancement or organisational change. This lets people know we feel it in our heart, mind and gut. Second, you also need to be aware of the emotional state of the people you are trying to persuade. Knowing this, you can adjust your message and tone to suit. Like corporate communication, it becomes a matter of knowing yourself and knowing your target.

> *It is also a mistake to confuse argument with persuasion.*

Common ground

Without common ground, you will not persuade. Your messages need to be framed so they appeal strongly to the people you want to persuade. You will only do this if you know what they are thinking, which means you have to listen to them. A common mistake is to focus totally on your own message, leaving no room for feedback, and thereby increasing the risk that your message will miss the target. The best persuaders have a keen interest in others and are able to listen.

Be dramatic

Facts do not excite people. They become a dry argument. We all look for some spark, some fizz in the message, so you will need to increase your presentation skills. Your messages become stronger if you tell them through anecdotes, personal reminiscences, stories and authoritative sources.

Create credibility

If you have credibility you can be persuasive. Generally, credibility comes from being good at what you do, being reliable and trustworthy and by building good relationships. Trust results from making commitments to do things, and then doing them. It also comes from telling the truth, always. Networking extends the influence of trusting relationships and becomes a broader platform for your persuasive skills.

Build teams

Team players and team builders are our favourite people. We like them, we listen to them and we allow them to persuade us. Every time you are in a group setting, try to contribute something that is positive and will make the group feel good. Being in teams also helps you learn to negotiate conflict, which is a good launching pad for persuasion.

The art of persuasion is something you can learn throughout working life. You will never perfect this art, so keep learning. We naturally associate with and listen to people we like. The more you can create a genuine interest in and caring attitude for others, the more you will be liked and trusted by them. Fear, on the other hand, keeps you isolated from people and firmly on the road to failure. Communication is all about liking and understanding people, creating the highway to success. If you communicate well, there is much less chance of being overlooked and a much greater chance of moving towards a better job.

A FAIR GO FOR WOMEN

In business life, we have to stop picking on women but, with many businesses addicted to old-fashioned management, change will be slow coming. A lot of this corporate picking on women comes in the form of being overlooked for promotion, while asking women to do more work and take on even greater loads. Ignoring the leadership strengths of women must have cost corporations a fortune, yet few shareholders have bothered to hold management accountable. In too many businesses, not enough women are listened to, promoted or respected. The end result is a loss to the profits and share value of the corporation. If the loss was from any other source, senior management would not tolerate it continuing and they would move in and fix the problem.

> *Ignoring the leadership strengths of women must have cost corporations a fortune . . .*

It is different in the professions where climbing the ladder has been possible for women and ability is better recognised than gender. The good news is that many women are completing MBAs and making it in business ranks. Despite some progress, not enough people at the top of business take a commonsense, good business approach to women employees. The glass ceiling is holding many women back.

Sarah, a good friend, studied part time at work for an MBA, a course she flew through with great results. Through all that study, she didn't miss a beat at work; her clients were well looked after and happy. More than that, the solutions Sarah provided for her clients made them better businesses; she was a real asset. Clearly, at her age, with her experience and qualifications, she was her employer's most outstanding prospect for future leadership. Within years she could have generated larger profits for that business. But her firm overlooked her for promotion, brought in male recruits from outside and placed them in senior positions. Familiar story? Moving to another location in the hope of fairer, more open treatment, she was given a review by her manager and was knocked back for promotion, with the warning, 'Sarah, you smile too much'.

What's happening here? The clue is in the 'You smile too much' comment. We have to start focusing on male leaders, and correcting what is wrong in their leadership. I've seen first hand that within corporations too many men do not enjoy their work, rarely have fun with it and are on a fast path to becoming grumpy old men. They have an MBA in moaning and frowning. They control the culture of the workplace, at least at the leadership level. The sooner they are helped out of this misery, the better. I know the next generation of employees, male or female, does not want to be inducted into this management 'hall of frown'. These grumpy leaders are the same ones who think the Internet is a gimmick, not a new marketplace. You can see the pattern. They don't like any form of change and everything is just another problem, just another headache. Not every male leader is like this; too many are. It is important not to heap blame on these leaders. Instead we should concentrate on ways to re-educate and revitalise their leadership.

Diane DiResta, President of DiResta Communications, USA, asks: are women cocreators of their own sabotage? She believes that the glass ceiling does exist, 'But women often help to keep success at arm's length by the way they communicate'. Now I agree that communication holds the key to success, but I am not impressed by those who suggest women should be tougher than men or, on the other hand, that they should cling to a 'nurture and emotion' formula. Learning communication from corporate PR is not about turning you into something you are not; it is about getting your message across so people know how good you really are. If we could all, men and women, communicate who we really are and what we can offer, surely that's good enough and glass ceilings would begin to crumble. My message to men and women is that by studying how corporations communicate, they can pick up the skills to evaluate where they are today, and how to advance their cause for tomorrow.

> *... I am not impressed by those who suggest women should be tougher than men ...*

Credibility killers

DiResta has developed a list of credibility killers that I think are useful for people in general, not just women.

Too much head nodding

My observation is that women nod their heads and smile more than men. What does this mean? When women nod they generally mean 'I hear you' or 'I understand you'; men, on the other hand, interpret nodding as agreement. In this way, communication is disrupted and confused. This suggests that DiResta's advice is good; too much of this head nodding may result in misunderstanding. But DiResta misses an important point. The reason people nod and smile is that they are open and communicative, so those who don't (generally men in management) should start nodding and smiling some more, so they receive better communication.

Uptalk

People will not be taken seriously if they have a rising inflection at the end of sentences. Why? This rising inflection sounds tentative, as if posing a question. The alternative is to practise bringing the voice down at the end of each sentence. Better speaking skills would help most people get their message across, and it is worth taking a course early in your career. Remember that how you say it can be as important as what you say.

Weak language

The problem here, according to DiResta, is the use of tag lines and modifiers. Tag lines are when we have made a good communication and then ask 'Don't you think?' or add 'right' at the end. 'So this is a good idea, don't you think?' is an example of a tag line weakening a statement that should have just been 'So this is a good idea'. Modifiers include 'Just a thought', 'Hopefully, you've got my message', 'I guess I would like to say' and 'I'm only a beginner'. Most audiences don't like modifiers, because they prefer to make their own judgments. These are good clues for everybody: weed out tag lines and use strong, simple language.

Allowing interruptions

DiResta believes men jump in and say what they think and interrupt more than women, whereas women are more likely to be cut off. I despair for a quick solution here, when so many in leadership believe management is not about relating to people, but about controlling them. There's a perception that women are not tough enough for management, so interrupting them becomes justified. On top of this, men simply do interrupt women: at work, in social groups and at the coffee shop. The collaborative style of management, so often considered to be a female style, brings out the best in people. Is the solution to train women to handle interruptions or to train men to respect people and to become better listeners? Meantime, a polite 'Please hold your questions or comments a moment' allows the speaker to finish the idea or concept.

Not speaking up
Some women, says DiResta, wait to be called upon or avoid making comments at meetings. Waiting holds back any career. It communicates lack of preparedness. Meetings need to be prepared for. It is best to make one solid contribution to every meeting you attend. If you are having trouble making a point at meetings, you had better learn to interrupt to have your say, because to be counted, you first have to be heard.

Dressing inappropriately
DiResta stresses the importance of visual impressions and that clothing and appearance are part of communication. DiResta wants women to avoid looking sexy at work; avoid low-cut blouses and micro-mini skirts. My view is that the key for clothing, male and female, is to reflect the right values for the job. Dressing one level above your current position is a good signal. For example, if you are a supervisor, dress like the managers. Dress for the situation. While a formal suit may be right in an insurance company, it seems out of place in an IT incubator. If you aspire to a more senior role, dress in the way the more senior people dress.

Too softly spoken
Nobody likes to strain to listen, and a soft voice communicates insecurity and lack of confidence. Some skills training, for women and men, can help you breathe properly, project your voice and gain the attention you deserve.

Allowing others to take credit for ideas
A common complaint from women, according to DiResta, is that men take credit for their ideas. Not surprising, since many men at the top have made an art form of taking credit for other people's ideas. She wants women to speak up and claim the credit. For example, say 'Excuse me, I just said that a minute ago'. I would be cautious about this, preferring to take the approach of making your recommendations loud and clear in the first place, so it is harder for anybody to claim them as theirs.

Weak body posture
Gestures such as shrugging shoulders, not making eye contact, standing with one leg crossed in front and a weak handshake weaken your impact, advises DiResta. Men are used to taking up more space and generally do, so it is important to stand tall, sit straight and act like you belong.

Avoiding public speaking
One of the biggest mistakes women can make, according to DiResta, is avoiding public speaking. It's a mistake many men have made down the years. Even worse are those who think they can speak, and then do an

appalling job. Public speaking is one measure of our future potential. Get some coaching, and do it.

The best managers I have seen (male and female) have been open, friendly, collaborative and noncombative. Almost all of these successful managers would have been even more successful by further refining their communication skills. I have also seen plenty of conflict lovers get to the top. Who will win in the future? My tip is that corporations of the future will see more real communication, more agreement and cooperation between people and a new style of leadership, where getting the message across will be a central management skill.

USING COMMUNICATION TO ADVANCE YOUR CAREER

How do the best executives use communication to advance their careers? Here are ten secrets applied from the top communicators I have seen. This list goes a long way towards answering the age-old question: what makes a good communicator?

Prepare messages

Good leaders always have a 'ready statement' of where the organisation is now, where it is going and how it will get there. They like their organisation. These leaders can use this ready statement at formal meetings or when they bump into someone in the foyer.

Address perceptions, not reality

Deal with what people think is happening. Top communicators know that what people think of them holds the key to their future. They like people. They have the confidence to listen to others and demonstrate respect by asking lots of questions.

Know yourself

Good leaders who are top communicators can sum up themselves and their company in a few sentences. Liking their organisation, they know their organisation well. Can you do that for yourself?

Explain capabilities

Good communicators can list their organisation's strengths and capabilities, as if it is a recorded message. They never tire of repetition, knowing that a message repeated is a message communicated.

Convert the complex to the simple

Successful people sum up complex things in simple language. The more technical their knowledge, the simpler their language.

Use the five Ws
The five Ws are who, what, where, when and why. The best executives answer the five Ws in the first sentences of a discussion or meeting. This way, they quickly sum up what they want to say.

Be practical
Good senior communicators are down to earth and practical.

Ask questions
The best business communicators are always asking questions. They are interested and inquisitive, because they like people.

Be purposeful
There is rarely any small talk for the top chief executives. They are not backward in making purposeful statements and rarely think, 'I wish I had said . . .'.

Make an impact
Top executives can grab the audience, then develop their message and close with impact.

Don't be alarmed when you read this list, because all ten points can be achieved by anybody. Just by thinking them through you will become a better communicator. Nobody can do this for you, so do it yourself. It helped me a lot early in my career to know that not many top executives are great and inspiring speechmakers—some of them are shy and quietly spoken—but they all apply most of these ten tips. These tips won't eliminate nerves or fear, but they can help you transform those energies into a more positive result. Gradually, these positive results build confidence and weaken your fear. Follow the ten tips to communicate better and advance your career.

12 LEADERSHIP IS ALREADY WITHIN YOU

Many people say they cannot apply the techniques of corporate communication because they do not have dozens of PR experts guiding the way. They look at leaders, and feel the art of leadership is out of their own reach. Even within corporations, many executives feel that PR is just for the PR department, so they don't bother refining their own skills. These people often miss out on promotion. Many community groups complain they can't get the message across because they don't have teams of writers. 'We could do better if we had a big PR department' is the cry.

Fortunately, this view is nonsense. It's just another fear, becoming yet another excuse for never creating better communication. 'I couldn't do that, I don't have the knowledge, I don't have the resources' is often stated but is rarely true. Almost all people can communicate better. Leadership, through better communication, exists within you, it just needs to be unlocked. You don't need loads of resources to do it. The size of a corporation's communications or PR department is not a reliable indicator of the effectiveness of its communication. While most large PR departments do add communication value, I have seen many large departments so confused and spread out that they have failed to communicate core messages. I have also seen huge companies with only one or two PR people achieving great impact with their messages.

> **Leadership, through better communication, exists within you . . .**

This is good news for you, and for your community. The tools of corporate PR can work effectively when handled by one, or by one hundred. It is just a matter of applying them confidently to your life or your community group. So, forget the excuses and learn how the best corporations communicate.

CHARACTERISTICS OF EFFECTIVE PR

Rather than worry about the size and budgets of corporate PR departments, I prefer to focus on the characteristics that make for good corporate PR. Having worked with dozens of corporate communication specialists, I have identified the characteristics defining those who succeed. Study these characteristics and you will become more of a leader. They can be applied to personal communication, at work or in the community.

Agility

Good corporate PR departments have the agility to adapt to changing conditions. In business, nothing stands still and very few things can be accurately predicted. It is the same in our daily life. At work you face constant change. Likewise, community groups face a constantly changing community, so they need to be agile in their communication. Leaders know when to drop something that is not working, or to pick up a new theme when the time is right. Our best corporations do not lock themselves into unchanging or inflexible positions. Why should you? The factors surrounding your life are just as changing and unpredictable as they are for corporations, so a good form of preparedness is to avoid being locked into strict responses. A good maxim is treat each new situation as a new situation. With flexibility, you can modify your position or your action, as you need to. If, on the other hand, you want life to stand still and are frightened by change, your communication will become dull and predictable, lacking the flexibility that inevitable change requires. I had this knee-jerk communication approach in my business prior to the introduction of computers. Everyone around me knew that 'a way to stir up Steve' was to talk about our need for computers. Automatically, I would trot out the same 'No way' response, quoting my experience as a journalist where we had to fight to get a typewriter. This learnt and habitual communication stopped me addressing the real issue: we needed new technology. Ultimately, the delay cost us money. An important lesson from corporate experience is that communication habits can become expensive.

> *...a good form of preparedness is to avoid being locked into strict responses.*

Focus

You can't be all things to all people. That is as true for community groups, clubs and individuals as it is for our biggest corporations. One characteristic of smaller PR departments is they recognise that they cannot effectively address every issue they face. Instead, they have systems that enable them to focus on those issues having the greatest business or financial market impacts. Wouldn't this focus be good in your career or in your community? Communities would talk more and participate more if they focused on what matters. Instead of being distracted by too many things, unable to ever resolve any of them, why not focus on one or two and handle them well? In improving your communication skills, concentrate on one aspect (such as asking more questions) at a time.

Learning from corporations, you will be more aware that, in effective communication, focus is a key to clarity and clarity is the key to getting your message across. Some of our best leaders have great patience, sticking to the one or two core messages that matter. They repeat themselves, time and again, appearing focused and strong. When you stick to the core message, you go to the heart of the matter instead of allowing your mind to make your communication jump all over the place.

Commonsense

The best corporate PR plans are often not exciting reading. You may be looking for the grand idea, the creative output or the big scheme. They are often not there in the best PR departments. Instead, they concentrate on providing value. They recognise the importance of being pragmatic and only doing what is necessary to accomplish the result. They understand overkill, watch out for empire building and apply commonsense to avoid them. Think of some of the best leaders and you will almost certainly think of commonsense. In thinking about your own communication, or that of your community, see commonsense as a big step forward to improvement. Do not feel you need something more than you already have: good, old-fashioned, intuitive commonsense is the best start in any communication.

> ... focus is a key to clarity and clarity is the key to getting your message across.

Promotion

When the best corporations communicate, the result is generally to promote themselves. They deliberately choose strategies that promote themselves and their goals, instead of just responding to external pressures or crises. They capture opportunities and promote as much as possible. In sporting parlance, they combine active communication offence with tough communication defence to ensure they always get their message across.

While this strategy is less suited to the home, it can work well for you in the community and in the office. It need not be as self-centred as it sounds. Being a promoter means that one of the thoughts you have in any situation is how to convey your message. It is not the only thought, but at work it should be one thought. Good leaders always know beforehand what they will say at that impromptu opportunity. Their themes are ready in their mind, and they never become bored with repeating themselves. By building an active communication offence, you will be known by more people and get your message across to

> ... see commonsense as a big step forward to improvement.

more. When people misunderstand you or what you are doing or stand for, it is time for communication defence. Offence and defence add up to promotion.

Relationships

Aren't some people great users? Are any of your friends guilty of expecting your support without earning it? Plenty, I'm sure. It is the same in corporate life. Good corporate communication realises the long-term value of regular communication and building enduring relationships. Having developed these relationships, the corporation knows they are there in time of need.

Relationships become a good protection. In the media, for example, a competitor may get a negative story run about you. If the journalist already had a relationship with your company, the competitor might have been knocked back. At least the journalist would have checked with you prior to publication. In this way, relationships become a form of protection.

Leaders value relationships, for they know that for them to lead they must have followers. They nurture and help others, thereby gaining trust and confidence. By building a wide range of relationships and working at them, you have the same form of protection and connection. It can be as simple as phoning a friend, now. Community groups are often users and many do not even realise it. For example, the garden club that only talks to the media when it wants to promote its annual fair is a user. That club would do much better if it also provided the media with seasonal gardening tips, even when it has nothing special of its own to promote.

One of my clients was his own best PR department. I helped him prepare the messages, but his own energy got the message across. His building supply business was always getting mentions on radio—in commentary and talkback form. My client made a point of phoning radio personalities and inviting them to lunch. He would also look for how he could help the radio personality. Some of this help might have offended my sensibilities (it might have been free building products, a free lunch or a free cruise) but it was how he did business. My client had front, which means he was not worried by knock-backs and just kept phoning his targets. Once in, he built relationships with the personalities, many of which lasted years. Being a world traveller, he would call from overseas and offer his colourful commentary on what was happening there at the time, so he became a bit of an on-air name. Behind it all was the planned desire to promote and build his business, using communication as a key to success. In communication, perseverance and bravery are well rewarded.

It is no excuse to look at the huge corporations and say they have all the riches and resources to communicate well. Much of what is achieved in corporate PR is best done by a few, and can be easily applied by individuals and community groups. Remember the key words: agility, focus, commonsense, promotion and relationships. They can all help you communicate better.

PART 3
Anger, crises, conflict and negotiation

13 **Dealing with anger** 91

14 **Overcoming selfishness** 101

15 **Survival aids in a crisis** 108

16 **Communication breakdown and barriers** 113

17 **Handling conflict** 119

18 **Gaining influence through communication** 125

DEALING WITH ANGER

The trouble with anger is that it becomes a shared emotion. It spreads. If we feel anger and say something angry to a friend or colleague, the chances are extremely high that they will also get angry. This then builds into workplace disagreements or family feuds. The whole thing can start inside one person, with their feeling of anger. Anger reminds us that communication can be positive and negative. When used by angry people, communication is a fearful weapon, building anger upon anger until everyone is fighting.

Anger, and steps to control it, provide a perfect example of my central view that creating positive outcomes from communication is based on two equally important ingredients: the mind and communication skills. Improving your mind without learning the skills will leave you with anger, as you continue to live with the acute frustration of never being able to get your message across or never being able to find the right words. Learning the skills but remaining dominated by the monkey mind of negativity is equally useless. Success comes from the right attitude and the right skills. In a society concerned about the growth of angry behaviour, from simple examples such as road rage through to tragedies such as mass shootings, we need to go back to the basics to find the way forward.

> **Success comes from the right attitude and the right skills.**

While most of us view anger as a strong and immediate emotion, it can also be a dull form of resentment, growing inside us. This resentment can be towards other individuals, or it can be a rejection of groups of people who don't think or look like us. For many, resentment comes from their own lack of material wealth, often blaming others for this 'failure'. Resentment seems to bubble inside, creating turmoil that prevents us from thinking clearly or seeing events for what they really are. Everything is traced back to our core of resentment, events seem to fit a pattern, and so the resentment grows. Many resentful people live with a victim mentality, constantly feeling helpless and seeing everything that happens as further proof of their own suffering. The situation worsens because the way we think does impact on events and on what we do, becoming a form of self-fulfilling prophecy.

This can have bad results at work, leaving you stuck in a junior or inferior role. It can have tragic results in marriages and families. Under the failure and anger syndrome, one partner burns inside with a sense of anger and sees every event and every statement from the perspective of that anger. Whenever their partner tries to help, the perspective distorts this positive action into something untrustworthy or confronting. So the arguments increase and the anger feeds on anger. The person generating the anger is convinced they are thinking straight: in their mind, they are suffering many hurts in life and have the idea that they can eliminate the pain if they reciprocate. It's a ridiculous notion, but totally convincing from their perspective—remember the importance of an individual's perspective in communication? The angry person will only change when they realise that when they get angry, they will suffer most. In this way, many people make themselves unhappy because of their reactions to events and situations.

The 'monkey mind' plays a role in building anger. It tells us that if we feel hurt in some way, the best response is to inflict pain too. Mostly this pain is inflicted on others, but many people react to hurt by inflicting more pain on themselves, condemning themselves further. They seethe inside, building resentment. Modern science is finding that this internalisation of stress and resentment not only creates isolation and unhappiness, it also contributes to physical illness, depression and lack of energy. Unless we become aware of the deception of this form of thinking, we will never change anger.

> ... it also contributes to physical illness, depression and lack of energy.

STRATEGIES FOR DEALING WITH ANGER

I am suggesting two ways to deal with anger: one is to go to the source (your mind) and the other is to learn new techniques from how corporations handle problems. Again, the solution involves the mix of mind and messages.

Dealing with an angry mind is the tough part. If your mind is angry enough to be causing obvious problems for yourself and others, it is time to seek some professional counselling so you can get on with a positive life. Do not hesitate or delay. If you think you have a problem with anger, chances are that it has been absolutely awful for those around you. So move now to fix it.

For most of us, anger is a part of life and we can benefit from being more balanced in our attitudes as problems arise. Life is constant change, and change brings problems, so we will be much happier and more effective if we change our response habits.

Some of the best advice is simple. Tulku Thondup Rinpoche has been a visiting scholar at Harvard University and has published many books on Tibetan Buddhism, including *The Healing Power of Mind* (Penguin, 1996). He reduces the complex to the simple, and here is his simple approach to dealing with anger:

> *If we are under great emotional pressure, it is best not to say or do anything. If you feel angry, excited or extremely happy, wait a while. Otherwise, what you say will be untrue or partially true, and likely to cause harm . . . the time to talk things over or make decisions is when we are calm.*

In workplace situations, a part of the calmer approach is to take a broader perspective, being aware of your own faults and thinking about what the other person is trying to do or say. Too often we just plough in and set off an emotional storm. It's a bit pathetic, isn't it? Here we are, with education and information, going crazy like a programmed toy whenever certain things are said or done. Most of the people we live and deal with will know what triggers our response. It's like a blockage that refuses to go away, meaning you hold yourself back. You suffer. Instead, think and wait. If there is a problem, think about what might have caused it. If you cannot think of the cause, don't worry, it might be too complex for you. Just accept that there is a problem and this will mean you tread carefully in your communication.

> **If there is a problem, think about what might have caused it.**

If we always see problems as being totally negative, it becomes habitual, and we will constantly be preoccupied with how painful and awful life is, turning even minor problems into huge obstacles. Instead, when we see a problem, we should take a breather, relax, and try to think slowly about what we need to do. If we can slow down enough, the problem will reduce in power and our brain will be clear to deal with it. Instead of a cluttered and hurried brain, we slow down to create a smooth and open brain. In this way we come to see problems more clearly. We minimise the chances of anger arising.

It is a good idea to practise thinking positively. Then, when problems occur, we do not automatically lash out in the old way. Practise if you find yourself standing in a queue. Instead of shuffling from foot to foot, with mounting impatience, see the queue as an opportunity for slow, deep breathing and a rare time to relax. If it is raining outside, instead of muttering as you reach for the umbrella, think of the rain as a key to life. If a car cuts in front of you in traffic, try to think of it as no more and no less than one small car length. That is, try to create a habit of making the best of a situation. These are small examples of what can become a real and lasting change in your thinking.

HOW CORPORATIONS SOLVE THE PROBLEM OF ANGER

Corporations get angry too. They experience problems and face the same choices we face: they can lash out and react angrily, or they can put a strategy in place to deal with the problem. We can learn from how the best and worst deal with problems.

The wrong approach

Let's start with what some of our worst corporations have done when problems occur. Think about whether any of these bad responses also apply to you. In my own consulting and research on crisis management, I have identified the four major negative corporate reactions to a problem or crisis.

Cover up

A bad corporation tries to cover up a problem, publicly pretending it never happened or burying their head in the sand in the hope that no-one will find out. The media always find out, sometimes many years later, and the result is an instant and long-term loss in confidence among investors, customers and suppliers. The company is in big trouble because it thought it could cover up a problem. Many small problems are turned into corporate catastrophes in this way.

Lash out in print

Aggressive senior management sometimes behave like prize-fighters, all red-faced and ready to throw a punch. The moment a problem arises, these corporations lash out at their competitors or governments or any ready target. They often race into print with full-page advertisements; generally wordy diatribes no-one ever reads. Lashing out in print is like formalising the argument, like setting it in stone. They waste shareholder funds, confuse the public and draw mighty amounts of attention to the problem, without letting us know what they will do about it. It is like shooting yourself in the foot and is the corporate equivalent of personal anger.

First, and often, take legal action

Because they see problems as an overwhelming negative, these corporate leaders use the law as their first point of refuge, instead of considering it as one of many options. They are often heard to say, 'We'll sue the pants off them'. Bluff and bluster are elements of their leadership style. One side effect of legal action is that today's problem lasts for years and years, as the courts and legal process take their time to consider the issue. It can magnify the problem, while it certainly prolongs it. Legal action may be warranted in certain cases and, of course, in some instances it can provide the solution we need, but bad corporations use it first and often, instead of reviewing all the alternatives.

Forget the staff
In their race into print and to the law, these corporations rarely stop to think about one of their greatest assets: their staff. Front-line staff are kept totally in the dark on developments and have no way to help communicate the corporate story. They cannot put the best corporate foot forward. They simply don't know what is going on, and feel uncared for and unwanted.

These bad corporations tend to have problems more regularly than most, because one thing they never do is change their behaviour. Because they tend to lash out and blame everyone else, they have little interest in improving their systems or processes. They are not concerned with eliminating the causes of problems, so the problems keep popping up.

Ivy Ledbetter Lee started work at the beginning of last century as a journalist and soon was one of two partners in a pioneering PR consultancy, Parker and Lee, created in 1905. He saw the mistakes corporations make in trying to be secretive. At the time he was operating, journalism was more of the muckraking kind, with business as the main target. So it was not surprising that many companies had a fear of disclosure and openness. This simply played into their hands, building a reputation for companies as secretive organisations, with little concern for public information. Contrary to this trend, Lee believed in supplying the newspapers with as much information as possible. His Declaration of Principles, drafted in 1906, explained his commitment to guaranteeing the accuracy of his facts and leaving to the discretion of the newspaper editor whether an item was worth printing as news; his aim was to provide news, not advertising. This logically led to his commitment that corporations should open themselves up for scrutiny, rather than try to avoid the media or keep secrets.

Lee practised these theories for the Pennsylvania Railroad in 1906. The railroad had a policy of refusing reporters access to all accident sites, and it never granted interviews. This policy led to substantial mistrust, with reporters obviously starting out on stories with the belief that the railroad was wrong and was covering something up. Their fear led them to appear guilty, every time. Lee opened the lines of communication with the media, providing frequent information updates. Importantly, he arranged for reporters to visit any accident sites, thus turning distrust into understanding.

The right approach

Good corporations are always much stronger and better after a problem has occurred. They learn from problems, they find solutions and work to improve themselves so that the problem does not arise again. You can learn from the experience of good corporations, finding new ways to control or manage your own reactions of anger, fear or conflict.

When good corporations face a crisis or a problem, they take these six steps:

- Get the facts.
- Communicate action.
- Review their stance and processes.
- Take market soundings.
- Change their behaviour and practices.
- Get the new message across.

The first step is to get all the facts around the problem, and this needs to be done with a cool head. Remember that the first casualty of war is the truth. So, the first casualty of a corporate crisis is the facts. Isn't this also true in our personal lives? Assembling the facts may take some time, but that does not stop the corporation communicating in the meantime; after all, the public needs to know that you are assembling the facts.

One example from PR illustrates this point effectively. An explosion occurred at an oil refinery, with loss of life. No-one knew what caused it, and the refinery had an excellent safety record. In this case, a bad corporation would have locked its CEO away in a room and sent out a written note citing its fine track record. But this was a good corporation, and the CEO went immediately to the refinery to hold a press conference. You can hear the lawyers and others warning the CEO not to say anything until he had all the facts. They missed the communication point. When a problem occurs, we want the corporation to acknowledge it and do something to fix it. So this CEO fronted the press. He expressed his dismay at the incident, stated his deep compassion for the families of the deceased, announced the formation of a fact-finding team and promised it would work day and night until the company knew what caused the explosion and could prevent future incidents. This was a marvellous piece of communication, but of course it was only the beginning of a long and difficult communication process. But it was a beginning.

> When a problem occurs, we want the corporation to acknowledge it and do something to fix it.

Communicating action goes well beyond holding press conferences. Good corporations try extra hard during a crisis to make sure all of their key audiences have the facts. These key audiences include staff, customers and suppliers. Letters are sent, executive teams are dispatched with presentations, meetings are held, phone

> Every effort is taken to ensure key people know what is going on.

calls are made. Every effort is taken to ensure key people know what is going on. If the issue involves the local community, the corporation could set up a communication forum, designed to give everyone a say, as well as providing a vehicle for factual information. This painstaking and careful communication produces much better results than merely placing a full-page diatribe in the newspaper. Applying this approach to your life, when a problem arises it is important to keep communication channels open. Avoid making hasty and negative statements but instead remain open to communication, keeping in touch rather than lashing out.

As the problem is revealed, the good corporation reviews its stance and processes, takes new action and communicates this to the public. Think about yourself and a close friend after a heated argument: you can really cool things down by seeing it partly from their side and acknowledging some part of what they have said. As you pause and wait, generally the other person will acknowledge part of what you said, and on it goes, putting the whole silly argument in perspective.

Corporations may also at this stage do some market research among key audiences so they have a clearer idea of what people are thinking. When communicating about a problem, it can be more important to know what people *think* happened than to know what really happened. People's perceptions are reality to them, so you have to communicate within those perceptions. This market research may involve staff, customers and suppliers and, for many, extend into the broader consuming public. For most of us, a small piece of market research would help when we face a conflict or feel anger rising. Why not just ask the other person what they are thinking, rather than make a big statement yourself?

People's perceptions are reality to them . . .

Changing behaviour and practices is a characteristic of a fine corporation, and one that is strengthened by a crisis rather than weakened by it. Any problem can be welcomed as an opportunity to look again at the corporation, review what it does and how it does things. Instead of blindly lashing out and blaming everyone else for the problem, good corporations learn from problems and change their behaviour. At a personal level, we might have contributed to the causes of our current conflict, and it is important to be open to this. Perhaps a change in your behaviour will reduce, not necessarily get rid of, the instances of conflict.

The job is not finished there for a good corporation, because long-term communication is needed when a crisis has hit. Long-term communication reinforces the positive change in the corporation, allowing it to move on from the problem into a new era of business. It does not get bogged down, unlike the corporation that tries to pretend a problem does not exist and many years later can still be dealing with it. Good corporations take action, communicate well and move on in life.

Much of this corporate experience can be applied to your life. Note that the bad corporation just lashes out in haste, while the good corporation takes its time and considers the situation. At a personal level, this suggests that patience is the key. When you face a problem, do not try to resolve it instantly. Rather, give yourself time to contemplate it. Instead of magnifying it, as the lashing out will do, taking your time over a problem can reduce its size and impact. Good corporations demonstrate a powerful way of controlling anger and avoiding the negative results of anger.

You can become more accepting (and less self-critical) of communication failure and, therefore, better able to move from the negative to the positive. When you do lash out, your understanding of communication will trigger awareness that you have slipped into the negative side and, with this awareness, you can take steps towards positive communication. Without awareness, you risk staying on the negative, angry side forever. When anger occurs, the communication is not satisfying; it is alienating and leads nowhere. If you know this, you can strive for satisfying communication that encourages responses and helps you move forward. Ignorance and anger probably support each other. Anger is like a backward step.

> When anger occurs, the communication is not satisfying . . .

DELIVERING EFFECTIVE APOLOGIES

What do you do once you have been angry? How do you apologise? Suppose you have thoughtlessly lashed out at a friend or work colleague. What is the best way to resolve this tension, acknowledge your mistake and move on?

If you have to deliver an apology, the first choice is how personal you should be. Face to face is the most personal, the most intimate. I would usually recommend that you choose this person-to-person approach to apology first. I have done this many times with clients where a conflict has occurred, say, between the media and my client. Nothing resolves it quicker than a short personal meeting, so that both sides can then get on with their work. In fact, normally after meetings like this they get on better than before. But we have many other ways to deliver messages today, and you should not instantly rule them out for apologies. These include a phone conversation, a voicemail message, a handwritten note, an email or a fax.

The choice can be difficult. Some people say that there is no match for the human voice, especially for sensitive messages. The voice carries so much more than the written word, they say, so they advocate that you deliver an apology in person or over the phone. Others think an email is more caring and more polite, because it does not interrupt the receiver, but instead gives them a chance to read and think before responding. The advantage of the voice is that it can give real emphasis, so your attitude is strongly conveyed. On the other hand, with written communication the apology is on the record. Why choose? If you have blundered into anger, why not use both? Delivering the message by word and by print gives you the best of both worlds, and the doubling up reinforces your sincerity and concern. My corporate clients always follow an important communication discussion with a written reinforcement of the message. You can use the same approach to apologising.

Do you know anyone who is polite and nice but becomes a real demon behind the wheel of a car? So it is with computers and telephones for some people. They hide behind the technology, becoming aggressive and bullying in ways they would not dream of doing face to face. It is important to remember that emails are quick and permanent, so think before you write and try to be calm before you communicate. An apology delivered in a flustered way could be counterproductive. Stop, think, count to ten—do anything to slow yourself down rather than send off an impulsive email message.

My advice to clients is to treat any written communication as a piece of public information. Clients see reason on this issue when asked, 'How would you feel if that letter was published on the front page of the morning newspaper?' If you would be comfortable seeing it published, fine, go with it. But if you would have any level of discomfort seeing your words in print, it is time for a rewrite after a rethink. Again, it is the ease and speed of emails that can lead you into unwise communication, so always take your time in print.

There are no hard and fast rules on how to deliver an apology. The most important thing is to deliver it. Corporations have learned the hard way that pretending a problem will go away is the best way to turn a small problem into a major and costly disaster. Saying you're sorry allows you and your friend to move on from the incident. A lack of apology keeps the incident alive, extending its impact over a long time. So if you have been angry, acknowledge it, apologise and move on without being too hard on yourself. You are not the first to lose your cool, and you won't be the last.

DON'T BE A PUSHOVER

Does overcoming anger mean that we let people push us around? Not if we are to judge from good corporations: they are not pushovers, but have a confident determination to solve problems. Do we let someone ruin a family function or spoil office harmony, simply because stopping them may involve getting a little heated and raising our voices? No. Is the alternative to anger to become a pushover? No. In fact, the alternative of patience and clear vision creates a stronger, more controlled individual who can apply a patient but effective response to the troublemaker. To communicate effectively we sometimes need to speak forcefully, while maintaining a non-angry attitude. This is really the reverse of shouting in an angry way and is much harder to achieve, but it gets results. Anger automatically corrupts what we say and do, producing outcomes we do not want. On the other hand, a calm and controlled mind can deal with a difficult situation in a positive way. It takes a combination of belief and learning: belief that anger is not a good emotion, and learning skillful communication techniques.

The social benefits of managing anger can be enormous, and may even have global impacts. As a minimum, reducing anger and resentment in our communities should mean we see more smiling faces when we walk down the street.

OVERCOMING SELFISHNESS

14

SELFISHNESS CAUSES COMMUNICATION BREAKDOWN

'Please don't let me be misunderstood' was a plaintive cry in a song I remember from the 1960s. Being a teenager at the time, I rather liked the sentiment of the song. We all want to be understood. Teenagers are not alone in being convinced they have no chance of being understood. In many offices, this complaint can be heard from people who feel the corporation is ignoring their pleas. In other cases, the selfish individual cannot understand why they have been missing out on promotion. In our homes, partners feel understanding is slipping away. Wherever it happens, the message is almost always the same: when communication is one-sided, when we only think of ourselves, communication breakdown always follows.

What causes this selfish approach to result in communication breakdown? Consider a friend of mine, Albert, a father deeply disturbed by his fifteen-year-old son, who was becoming something of a rebel after being the perfect child. The change was rapid—suddenly the son started staying out late, talking back, swearing and dodging school. Albert was confused and a little angry. Perhaps his son was just being a boy of fifteen? Perhaps at that age he should have been given some room to grow. As a minimum, perhaps he was too old to be heavied by his father. Albert explained to me how he could not control his own responses, that something triggered his overwhelming desire to show his authority and bring the boy into line. So, the scene kept repeating: again and again he would lay down some new rule or other, knowing that it would not work. It was at least a daily event, and sometimes occurred many times in one day. There was a nasty battle of wits between father and son. Albert found he was drinking a little more, staying at work a little later, and when at home he was often silent and sullen. Where once he and his son cuddled and laughed, they now felt like total strangers.

Why did Albert set out on this course of communication knowing it would not work? Why choose a course that may make things worse? It certainly wasn't because this was a considered response designed to improve things. The answer has a message for all of us. Albert had actually given in to a selfish need to do it, no more, no less. At that time he could think of nothing but himself and his own point of view.

Thinking of self, there was no room to think of his son. Communication went straight out the window as his self-righteous anger took over. Before you judge this father too harshly, consider when you might last have done the same, to a friend, at work or at home. It is so easy to say something merely because it will make you feel better, knowing that as an act of communication it could fail or even produce worse results.

HOW CORPORATIONS OVERCOME SELFISHNESS IN COMMUNICATION

What is the alternative? Application of a little corporate communication could improve our workplaces and family life. Why? Because corporations first consider who they are talking to before they say anything. Paramount in their mind is what the other person (customer, client) is thinking. Unlike Albert, who was just thinking of himself, these corporations think first about their customers or targets. They ask questions to make sure they know what these people are thinking. Then they only speak in a way the customers can understand and readily agree with. They speak their language. Then they check that the message has been received, by asking more questions or evaluating customer actions. It's a complete circle that requires thought before talk, question before comment and calmness before anger. This can become a useful motto on the office wall or on the fridge door, particularly if you are known for losing your cool and ranting and raving to little effect:

> *... these corporations think first about their customers or targets.*

- Thought before talk.
- Question before comment.
- Calmness before anger.

The selfish desire to say what is on one's mind regardless of the consequences happens all the time. We all seem to do it, some more than others. It's also something of a social disease. We hear it all the time: 'Then I really ripped into him. I know it went totally over his head but it made me feel better'. Did it make you feel better, really?

Taking the concept further, what convinces a minority group within a trade union that a violent protest against the corporation will help their cause? The violent protest takes focus away from the real issue, such as the legitimate case for a pay rise or improved safety, and makes people wonder about the wisdom of unions. No thought is generated for the issues at stake. The action has blinded us to the very message that it was hoped we could see. So why take this action? Because of the selfish desire to do what pleased themselves. Surely, their enraged minds said, violence would be nothing in comparison to this injustice. Won't people understand this? No, we do not. These groups, just like the father of the teenager, have forgotten about getting the message across and have become concerned only with their own feelings of anger or resentment.

I was once promoting a community cycling group that wanted a safe riding track built through the suburbs, keeping the riders away from the busy main roads. One of my hardest tasks was to convince the activists to drop plans for a blockade and demonstration. Their idea was to win public support by deliberately blocking the peak-hour traffic with a demonstration. I told the group that such an action would confuse their message and create outright hostility among many people who would otherwise be supporters of the move for a bike track. Most of the motorists we would be holding up lived in their suburb too. Many rode bicycles and would support the cause if they were not antagonised by being held up in traffic chaos. We eventually dropped plans for the blockade, and thought smarter. We held 'ride a bike' days, put on a sausage sizzle with local councillors and handed out positive community literature. We also found out that the mayor's children were keen riders and got them along to our functions. In other words, we created a friendly dialogue instead of a conflict.

There's a part of most humans that wants us to become irrational, to display a negative emotion in the hope that we will feel better while everyone else feels bad. This is poor communication and never produces the result you want. It never changes others' behaviour and only locks people into more stubborn positions. Our communication can be negative and ineffective or positive and rewarding. Think of the last personal communication you had with a work colleague, a partner, your teenage child, your parent or a friend. How did it go? By doing a feedback test every now and again, you will become more aware of how communication is going in your important relationships. It gives you the opportunity to correct the balance, to swing things to the positive. Otherwise, important relationships can seem to be always going out of control. It can be hard to do this test in an instant, so you have to trust your judgment and hope that communication will work in that moment.

> *It gives you the opportunity to correct the balance, to swing things to the positive.*

Selfish desire can overtake us all, as it did the father of the teenager. One way to stop is to check the emotions and, if they are rising, ask some questions instead of making statements. Again, this advice is based on my corporate experience. A leading insurance company was attacked by residents of a high-income area. The residents had gone off about some rumour and were way wide of the facts. Instead of countering with the facts (and risking getting the residents more off side), the insurance company started with some market research; that is, it listened to the other side. Only then did it prepare its communication, and as a result did so in a way the local community could readily accept. Questions are friendly, involve the other person and give you time to think and the emotion time to subside.

In the case of the father, after we had worked together for a while, he developed his own techniques for self-control. One was, in the car on the way home from work, to create pictures in his mind of his son as a baby, as a toddler, playing with him in the park and so on. With the feelings these mind pictures created, he approached his son with warmth and friendship, instead of tension and aversion. Feelings of warmth and friendship towards others can lay the perfect foundation for communication at home, at work or in the community. These feelings will certainly keep selfish anger at bay.

I've attended many corporate stress management sessions, and here is my adaptation of some of the best messages to help you control stress and minimise selfish outbursts:

- Take breaks, stand up, breathe deeply, be alone and slow your thoughts.
- Make life simpler—too much stress comes from trivia.
- Use delays positively—when caught in traffic, breathe deeply.
- Do something each day that you really like to do.
- Force yourself to talk over difficult things—once you start, it becomes easier.
- Learn how to say 'No' in a positive, friendly way, not in a way that closes doors.
- Take a walk, use the stairs, go outside at lunchtime.
- Do unpleasant tasks now—it takes less energy than worrying all day.

CAN YOU PLEASE SHUT UP?

People who talk too much are not good communicators. This goes against what many of us think, but there is a strong view among experts that people who talk constantly have a real fear of communication and suffer from low self-esteem. If you suspect that you or a friend do talk too much, take a look at what contemporary corporations are saying and doing about advertising, and apply this learning to your own personal communication or career development.

A marketing guru friend of mine (let's call him Jim) found the simple truth that people screen out unwanted messages. Jim reckons that we now have such a saturation of media messages that, in order to maintain their sanity, people have to screen things out. This can lead to pretty garbled and confused accounts of what they have seen. Since garble and confusion are the enemies of communication (and of happiness), you can learn lots here.

Leading packaged goods company, Proctor & Gamble, has said that when their message is deep and on target, when the consumer understands what they're doing and the message has resonance, then they're very confident their expenditure will build brands and pay dividends. The lesson here is listen to your audience, speak their language and get their attention. That's what good advertising does, and you can do it too. Good listeners are generally good communicators.

Can you learn to shut up and listen? Yes, you can learn the vital listening techniques that provide the key to effective communication. But you need to watch out, because even listening has some pitfalls. Misunderstandings are created by wishful listening, hearing only what you want to hear. The best tip for improving your listening skills is to remember to ask questions. That at least should force you to stop talking and give the other person a go.

> **The best tip for improving your listening skills is to remember to ask questions.**

In corporate training programs I have set out three different types of listening skills: empathetic, analytical and guiding. To listen with empathy, imagine yourself in the other person's shoes and try to understand what they are getting at. Make them feel good and comfortable and pay close attention to what they are saying. With empathetic listening, nod your head often as they speak. Analytical listening is where you ask specific questions to discover the thinking behind a person's statements. It's good to seek concrete information or to ask the other person to give a specific example of what they mean. This helps you analyse their comments. Guiding listening is more manipulative, where you want the other person to come to a certain conclusion. In this form of listening, your own statements should invite their ideas on specific topics, or your questions should include a specific solution so the other person can respond as if it is their own.

Once you are in a dialogue, it is important to take statements at face value and not read hidden or sinister meanings into what is being said. You can test your understanding of the other person's comments by rephrasing them and repeating them to the speaker. Good questions and statements to create understanding in this context are:

- ■ 'I'm sorry, I didn't catch the meaning of what you said. Would you mind repeating it, please?'
- ■ 'I would be very interested to hear your opinions about . . .'.
- ■ 'I know I have made this point badly. What I meant to say was . . .'.

Asking questions is fundamental to good communication. Powerful words you can use are: why, how, what and when. Use these words often to lift a one-sided conversation into a genuine, two-way process.

As well as knowing when to shut up, simplicity is important. Simple messages are easiest to understand. The top advertising slogan of the twentieth century was DeBeers' 'Diamonds are forever', with Nike second with 'Just do it' and Coca-Cola third with 'The pause that refreshes'. Each one is a simple, no-nonsense description of the product. This is not to suggest that in ordinary life you should speak in advertising slogans. But you can learn from corporate experience: listen to your target audience; create a simple, descriptive message, and then stick to it. That way, you avoid talking too much, while increasing the power of what you do say.

We all know the character who talks too much. They come round to dinner and open up with a speech on the death of football. You move the subject to the economy and they know the solution to interest rates. They advance their latest theories on politics and, after your child interrupts the meal, they share their knowledge of the five stages of child growth, followed by an environmental discourse and lecture on the ozone layer. It's boring.

> **When communication is always one-sided, it is not communication at all.**

Why are people who talk too much bad communicators? First, because they do not give you a chance to speak. They do not listen. Their primary interest must be themselves. None of us likes this. We don't like communication where people talk over us, because the result is alienating and not satisfying. There is no room for response. It therefore leads nowhere. When communication is always one-sided, it is not communication at all. But when there is room for feedback, the communication satisfies everybody involved and people get a chance to be responsive. As a result, we can move forward based on this shared experience.

The trouble with people who talk too much is that their mind is probably out of control, with thoughts all over the place, racing around, lacking confidence, fearful and closed off from others, always imagining things with ceaseless mind chatter. The monkey mind is in full swing. I've seen it hold back corporate careers, and it will hold back your personal communication. You can only achieve good communication if your thoughts are reasonably controlled, you feel some sense of self-assurance, you are open and friendly, and you slow down enough to see things as they are. Then you have a chance of getting the message across.

If you find that you are constantly afflicted by the jumping chatter, it may be because you are not happy. Think about this: do you always feel desperate for a change? Do you feel that most of the time people do not understand you? Are you thinking too much of yourself, always feeling you have missed out? If so, it is no surprise that your messages do not get across. You talk too much because you cannot risk silence. Silence might expose your nervousness or, worse, allow others to expose it for you. My reading of successful communicators is that they have a sense of personal happiness, based on a feeling of having what they want, which is that people understand them. These good communicators tend to think of others, and when they think of themselves it is with some sense of achievement and contentment.

Lack of personal happiness, then, can be a platform for poor messages: confusing to others, often delivered in a roundabout or almost deceitful way, always varying and all over the place. By shifting to a happier frame of mind, messages have a chance to become sharper, more focused, honest, simple and consistent and to hit the mark. People know what you are on about, what you want and what you stand for.

If you suspect that you are talking too much, it can help to convince your mind that you really like the person opposite you. Before you know it, you will have asked them a question and be listening intently to their answer. That is a start. Real communication is happening when two people are talking, not one.

> **You talk too much because you cannot risk silence.**

To promote yourself, you will have to stop thinking about yourself. The best communicators and the most successful people have got there because they always think first of the other person. They listen and are responsive, have stopped thinking of their own needs and are seen to relate to others. Sure, we can all think of examples of people who got to the top and were clearly selfish. Few of these succeed when they get to the top; their victory is short-lived. Genuine success comes from real communication; real communication comes from thinking about the other person before you think of yourself.

15 SURVIVAL AIDS IN A CRISIS

Problems come out of the blue. Very few corporations ever see a corporate restructure, merger or other radical change coming. In our personal life, most of us like things to stay as they are, so long as they are going well. Yet everything changes. This makes it tough on managers, but some of the best have an open approach to change and a commitment to communication. These are two very good defences.

In business life, the person who resists change is quickly run over. At a personal level, when we are in a good relationship, if we do not want it to change, we are disappointed when it inevitably does. Our partner develops new interests. Children grow up. Team-mates find new activities. In everything we do, there is change. The key is not to worry that you did not see the change coming. Instead, welcome the change and communicate your position. For most of us, our knee-jerk reaction to change is to oppose it. The best corporate managers that I have consulted to have all accepted that they work in a changing business world, they expect the unexpected and progress through change. You can learn from them.

> ... welcome the change and communicate your position.

COMMUNICATION SURVIVAL TIPS

Here are my communication survival tips for those who find themselves in the middle of vast change, whether personal or organisational.

Bide your time

When change hits, first watch and wait. Don't instantly scream in protest, or climb on the change bandwagon too early. Fear can make you strike out, even if you know this will ultimately hurt you. In many corporations, those who mindlessly jump on change are as dispensable later as those who oppose it. Any big change will involve some give and take, some adjustment and some winning and losing. So, learning from corporate experience, the first survival step is to do nothing: bide your time.

Solve problems

When it is clear what is happening, good managers consider the change plan in front of them and seek out opportunities to make a valued contribution. This may be by identifying weaknesses in the plan and providing solutions. The corporate truth is that it is best to be known as a problem solver, not as a problem.

Avoid gossip

I've heard it said that loose lips sink careers. When a corporation is in the middle of a major change, such as a merger, it is a highly charged environment. Some people will get better jobs, others will be out of work. I have seen experienced, senior people, when faced with change, spend all their time leaking information and talking about others. This gossip is unproductive, negative communication. Gossips generally find that their trusted colleague has immediately told others what they thought were private thoughts, as the grapevine goes to work. In your private life, apply a test to all communication in times of crisis by asking yourself 'Will this statement help the situation?'. If unsure, leave it unsaid.

Don't wallow in it

When corporations change, plenty of people will be hostile to the change and many will lose out. Stay away from the doom-and-gloom sessions because this can send the wrong signals to those above. Remember, they are stressed too. If they see you wallowing in it, even if your intention is only to give comfort, they could think that you have taken the opposition's side. Suddenly, you are cut out of further important discussions and your influence declines. The message from corporate experience is offer sympathy where it is useful, but avoid wallowing in it.

Help others

Good managers listen to their staff. They share all the information they can, and try to stop gossip and rumours by putting out the facts. They know that their behaviour will be mirrored by their staff. If they see change as frustrating, others around them are more likely to take a negative view. Good managers focus on helping others in times of change, replacing fiction with fact and negative with positive.

Jump in

Discussing his career, a colleague remarked on how much of the progress he had made was totally unpredictable. His approach was simple: every time he was offered a chance to participate in any corporate change, he took it. This kept him in the information loop and maintained his ability to influence events. This enthusiastic approach could give your career a boost.

Be positive

Corporate change can be seen as a negative or it can be viewed as a new career opportunity. It is the same in personal life. Change can be seen as a threat to you or as an improvement to your life. A positive, creative approach, well communicated, can help you carve out a new role. The alternative could be to let yourself become a victim, if only in your mind. Picking up from corporate strategies, for your career the best approach is to seriously consider why the change is taking place and how you can reinvent yourself to ensure the change is for the better.

DEALING WITH HOSTILITY

Sometimes hostility will occur face to face, and this makes it hard to remain positive. When somebody is red in the face, has an angry expression and is shouting about your failures, most of us have trouble staying calm. It's the same for public speakers and you can pick up some tips from them. For many speakers, the most frightening part of the presentation is the question and answer session at the end. What if someone becomes hostile? In this situation, it is the way you listen that really counts. Good listening is a skill that can be learned. It is your most active form of defence when under attack.

> *A positive, creative approach, well communicated, can help you carve out a new role.*

One simple approach to handling hostile comments or questions is to paraphrase the question or comment. You reply by saying, 'So, what you're saying is that this doesn't work and ... is that right?'. The other person's likely response is 'Yes' and you suddenly have them agreeing with you. Keep going. Dialogue is happening, and dialogue is always better than hostility. You can go further with this technique; you can paraphrase what they said but then ask for some clarification, such as 'So that is your most urgent need, right?'. This is seen as a step to sort things out. It gives the other person an opportunity to speak more calmly. Highly skilled speechmakers go further than this by using empathy ('Oh, yes. I've been there too. In 1998 my company sacked half the staff and we ...') or by highlighting the core emotion of the person. For example, if the hostile attack has been about your failure to deliver a report that answered all the key points, you could start your response with: 'That makes you feel that my team is not putting in while yours is wearing all the pressure. Is that it?'. This form of response needs some skill but it can leapfrog hostility into a real discussion, turning crisis into opportunity.

> *... it is the way you listen that really counts.*

CORPORATE CRISIS COMMUNICATION

Peter Drucker is known as the inventor of the field of management studies and has spent over three decades at the cutting edge of management thinking. He highlights the problems and difficulties of communication. His book *Managing in a Time of Great Change* (Plume, 1998) acknowledges that if we don't communicate well today, we don't get to do the things we want to do. Drucker says:

> We are one hundred years past the simple economy in which most people knew what others did at work. Farmers knew what most farmers did, and industrial workers knew what other factory workers did.

In my view, Drucker has highlighted one of the greatest causes of friction, hostility and crisis in our modern working lives: very few of us know what other people in our workplace actually do, yet we know we depend on each other. This goes further: very few parents know any more what their children are studying at school and college, and if they try to find out it turns out to be too complicated. Ignorance causes friction. Drucker continues:

> ... if we don't communicate well today, we don't get to do the things we want to do.

> But now no one knows what the others do, even within the same organisation. Everybody you work with needs to know your priorities. If you don't ask and you don't tell, your peers and subordinates will guess incorrectly.

How do you get started on these difficult conversations? We may know that a conversation will end a crisis, but not know how to get started or what line to take. My study of corporate crisis communication found that the first thing to go was the facts; in a crisis, suddenly no-one seems to know the facts. It's the same in a hostile conversation. Do you notice that in most arguments there is a big disagreement about the facts? The argument cannot move on to resolution because both sides keep harping on facts that the other side disputes. It goes nowhere. This form of argument happens in tennis clubs, at work and in homes.

> ... in a crisis, suddenly no-one seems to know the facts.

My advice is to ignore the facts. Instead, try to find out what is important to the other person. This leads to what they want, what they intend and what should be the outcome of the dispute. This is so much more productive than another round of argument about facts; the 'he said, she promised, they failed, we agreed' type of listing of so-called facts. Corporations will use this approach well in disputes, but they go further. Good corporations try to evaluate what is at stake in the argument and whether what is at stake really matters anyway. Often they find it does not matter, and they can easily concede, let go and move on. This is not a bad tip for personal relationship disputes. To do this, you don't waste time sticking to your own story. Instead, you find out what the other person's story is and evaluate its importance. These techniques won't avoid the need for difficult conversations and they won't stop conflicts, but they do move you to positive resolution. Otherwise, the dispute festers into a crisis and nobody can solve it.

Good corporate communication strategies are based on the inevitability of change. Nothing is expected to stand still; relationships are anticipated to be moveable. Few corporations criticise competitors, because tomorrow they could be working together. When celebrating this year's profit, they do so in a way that allows for the unpredictability of the future. While building the profile of a senior executive, they are aware the person may be poached by the opposition or walk under a bus. Rather than fearing change, they accept it as part of corporate life. That's why the best are ready for it when any change hits. You can be ready too. Effective communication is important all the time, but it is even more essential in a time of change.

Some change, such as the death of a loved one, seems so massive that you think you will never recover. But you can recover, even from the biggest loss. It all comes back to your attitude to change. If you accept that from the moment we are born we all change and ultimately die, then you are better able to cope with the inevitable changes of life. You will replace negative fear with positive concern. You may not know what the change is but when it hits, if you apply the above lessons, you can ensure a positive outcome through effective communication.

> **Rather than fearing change ... accept it as part of corporate life.**

COMMUNICATION BREAKDOWN AND BARRIERS

16

COMMUNICATION BREAKDOWN

Communication breakdown plays a part in every crisis and failure. This rule applies to couples, families and communities, as well as to companies. By looking at companies that fail (and I've seen a few), we can identify some lessons to help any of us when times are tough. A key to success is to accept that you will face communication breakdown, probably fairly regularly. Corporations expect there to be times when their messages don't quite get across. Of course, they would prefer to have perfect communication, so when things go wrong, they analyse why and change their communication strategy. Don't be surprised or depressed about it when communication breakdown hits you, but instead work to turn breakdown around. You can learn a lot about communication breakdown from corporations.

> *... accept that you will face communication breakdown, probably fairly regularly.*

Companies heading for failure have either stopped listening to their customers or never really learned how to listen. Often at the top were one or two key leaders who were used to being bullies, or had a reputation for hard-hitting toughness. These people often did not even like customers, let alone listen to them. They regarded most of their customers as 'dumb' and spread their own form of misery across everyone who came in their path. Praised in the 1980s, most of these so-called success stories lost lots of money, and until they became happier with themselves were doomed to long-term failure.

As profits dive and trading declines, in the absence of real feedback, these 'miseries' become defensive, even aggressive. An 'us versus the world' culture sets in. This is sometimes called a 'bunker mentality'.

Because the company wants to survive, they take steps to correct the slide, but because they do not have the skills to listen to customers, the steps they take are counterproductive. You hear them say, 'We've tried advertising and PR and they don't work'. True, advertising and PR based on your guess of what customers are thinking, rather than on truly listening to customers, are unlikely to work. They say 'If we could just get a decent sales force, we'd move product', without realising that they already have a decent sales force, they just did not have decent leadership. To make things worse, their internal communication systems break down, as the defensiveness and aggression increase. Their door is firmly shut.

Finally, they blame everyone around them and alienate the people they really need: their employees and their customers. Customers get so fed up they can't even bother to complain any more. They just go somewhere else. Sound familiar?

Why communication breaks down

Communication breakdown affects all companies, community groups, sporting clubs and families at some point. Taking lessons from corporate experience, here are seven main reasons for a breakdown in communication.

Letting rumours beat facts
If you don't put a lid on rumours, they become stronger than the facts. The best way to control rumours is to use strong, simple language within the group. A major cause of rumours is lack of real communication in the first place. In the absence of good communication and information, people fill the gaps themselves. This is where rumours become a real sign of communication breakdown. If a lot of rumours are surfacing within your business or community group, don't blame the gossips; act to improve group communication.

Communicating without one-on-one discussion
If there is something important to say, first prepare the group by talking one on one with people, so they are ready for the big announcement. This is called preparing the groundwork and it makes your audience more receptive to what is to come. It also allows you to know most of the likely objections in advance.

Lying
Lies create distrust. While there are always some things you just can't talk about because they're under discussion, you need to be careful how you keep these secrets. Communication becomes negative if you are known to lie on big issues. Distrust is not a good starting point for effective communication. There are times when it is best to say 'No comment' or admit that you can't talk about it right now.

Saying not doing
Actions speak louder than words. Communication needs to be underpinned by action. If all people hear is talk, or your actions show the opposite of what you say, they will believe the actions, not the words. Just as a picture is worth a thousand words, so your actions will always communicate more powerfully than your words.

Talking 'down' to people
Communication breaks down between people when one side thinks the other is stupid. If you respect people, you will acknowledge their right to know and their ability to understand. Your communication will be better if it grows out of respect for people. If you have something important to announce, don't gloss over parts of the message because you assume the 'dumb' members won't understand. It is much better to tell the whole story and allow them to ask about areas they did not follow.

Sending messages the wrong way
Communication can occur through many channels and it often breaks down because you have chosen the wrong one. For example, it may be counterproductive to send an apology by email when the person will really only respect you if you do it face to face.

Being silent
Steven Robbins, President of VentureCoach.com, writing for the Harvard Management Communication Letter, reinforces my concern about the risks of silence:

> *What you don't say may be sending as loud a message as what you do say. If you don't give praise, people get the message they're unappreciated. If you don't explain the rationale behind decisions, the message is that you don't trust them. And if you don't tell people where the company is going, they don't know what to do to help it get there.*

Robbins concludes with this useful advice:

> *If you're not regularly sending the messages you need to send, start now. And ask what messages may have been sent by your silence so far. Make sure you're giving people feedback on what to do and what not to do. And be willing to ask people: what messages are you getting from me?*

Communication breaks down more often than not because people say nothing. What they do not realise is that silence sends powerful, mostly negative, messages. In companies, families and groups, it is important to communicate

> **... silence sends powerful, mostly negative, messages.**

regularly and to give it real priority. If people do not get regular feedback they will make assumptions. Silence can be a real danger and is a potent contributor to communication breakdown.

The corporate approach to communication breakdown

In any communication breakdown, corporate or personal, the minds of the people play a key role. Where people's thoughts are all over the place, they lack confidence and they are closed off and fearful. Corporations are aware that their mind can play a negative role, so they begin by assembling all the facts and making sure everybody knows them. This can work for you, in your career and at home. What corporations do is like taking a breathing space to make sure you have got everything right. If you are aware that your performance is affected by your mental attitude, you will have some chance to move your mind to a point where thoughts are more controlled, and as a result you will feel more self-assured.

One of the best lessons from corporate PR is that their aim is always to increase communication and reduce conflict. By contrast, as individuals we often get hung up on who's in the right and this preoccupation makes us blind to ways of reducing conflict. By applying this corporate experience, you should start out with a mind that is open and friendly, giving you a greater chance to see things as they really are. This is a platform where real communication can flourish.

In most situations of communication breakdown, all the corporation wants is a solution so they can get on with business. Applying this to your situation, by looking for solutions instead of focusing on blame, real communication can be quickly restored. When you are negative and focus on blame, people don't understand you, leading to poor communication and ultimately to a further breakdown in communication. Communication breakdown is most comprehensively turned around when your mind is positive and looking for solutions.

Tony Rasman trained as a lawyer before becoming a PR consultant in Sydney. He is now the head of Fleishman-Hillard Stratcom's Litigation PR Unit. Tony knows the cycle of crisis and conflict and notes that most companies work well in phase one, putting their crisis team into action to manage the incident. They also do quite well on phase two, communicating with the public to defend the product and the company against allegations. But it is in the final part of the cycle that Tony believes many companies have much to learn—and we can learn here as well. When the crisis is settled and over, it is time for a company to restore confidence, yet many crisis teams pack their bags before the healing process has begun. This leaves a bruised and battered company trying to cope with the future. Instead, the team that helped it survive the conflict should also help it begin the process of winning back market share, rebuilding reputation and loyalty to the brand.

The lesson here, at the individual level, is that once a communication breakdown has been resolved, you need to work really hard on your communication to make sure the message does get across in future. It is easy to slide backwards.

Studies of good corporate leaders show that they spend a lot of time in discussions with their people. Philip J. Harkins, President of Linkage Inc., an organisational development company, writes in his book *Powerful Conversations: How High Impact Leaders Communicate* that 'All leaders talk'. He describes leadership as a series of conversations with anyone who can influence the success or failure of the organisation. Harkins says that leaders should make sure that every conversation they have results in three outcomes: advancement of an agenda; shared learning; and a stronger relationship. Much of this is based on honesty, which builds trust, an essential starting point for any effective communication.

BARRIERS TO COMMUNICATING THE NEW

The Gallup Organisation has extensive knowledge of how communication breakdown occurs and has compiled a list of seven things that restrict the communication of new information or ideas. These seven barriers are:

- **It's just too complicated**. The more complex the idea, the less likely we are to understand it or take action.
- **It's outside my knowledge**. People don't accept new ideas or new products if they are radically different from what they already know.
- **Accepted wisdom**. New ideas have to compete with already accepted ideas, and these can be so strong that new ideas fall by the wayside.
- **There's no proof**. Ideas are more readily accepted if they can be demonstrated and proved.
- **The vested interests are anti**. Vested interests can block a new idea by consistently getting their opposing message across.
- **I don't need it**. If we feel something is not needed, we won't budge.
- **What was that?** The public needs constant, frequent reminders of new ideas.

The message here is not to give up. Communicating new information or situations can be difficult but it is also a key to longer-term happiness. Otherwise, people will keep you in a corner. Like most of communication, when dealing with something new it is vital to listen to others, be clear about yourself, know what you offer, speak their language and provide plenty of chances for people to give you feedback. You might need to try, try again, because the barriers to communication can pop up when you least expect them. But that's no reason not to have a good go.

Follow these steps to effective communication, ridding your personal life and career of the heavy baggage of that old failure communication. Even if success is not immediate, you will at least be happier.

HANDLING CONFLICT

17

I've observed two kinds of conflict in corporate life: one that occurs spontaneously, and the other that builds over time. The first is a kind of communication explosion, which hits suddenly, surprising you as it totally takes over whatever you were doing. The second can take days or weeks to happen, and we may even know that it will ripen into conflict at a certain time, on a specific day. These two are very different forms of conflict. To communicate well in both situations requires different preparation but, fundamentally, conflict and hostility are just forms of communication, so be careful what message you are getting across.

Spontaneous conflict seems to occur more often at home or in sporting clubs, where suddenly an argument is happening. Often we have no idea where it came from, yet we have a powerful drive to become involved. If you find yourself caught up in this unpredictable conflict, the best form of defence is to change your attitude towards people. Most of us are constantly making mental judgments about others and we vary our approach based on these, often false, judgments. Try changing your attitude to a warm and friendly feeling towards everyone. Think of everybody you meet as someone just like you. Think how much you both share the drive for happiness, and how much you both want to avoid pain and misery. By cultivating a warm and friendly outlook, you will be less likely to be drawn in to spontaneous conflict.

> *Think of everybody you meet as someone just like you.*

The other form of conflict builds over time and this is the most frequent to occur in workplaces. John, a career executive in an insurance firm, actually had his promotions stalled because he gained a reputation for nastiness at meetings. In his insurance company, major projects were handled by committees. John's problem came about because, in between meetings, he would store away in his memory little points of niggling disagreement with other committee members. These would accumulate and spill out in conflict and hostility during the next meeting. Once he realised what was happening (with some help), he recognised that he had fallen into a conflict communication trap and set about changing his behaviour. In hindsight, he was a role model for controlling the mind and thereby creating a platform for positive communication. Whereas before his thoughts were all over the place, with the change they became more controlled; instead of being closed off from people, fearful of responses, he became more open; rather than imagining things, he came to see things as they are. For a start, when something annoyed him at work he dealt with it immediately, either by thinking it through and tossing it out of his brain as trivial or by raising his concern straight away and in private. His committee communication became positive and friendly, and promotion followed.

A part of overcoming conflict is to accept that what you are thinking will come out through your speech. It may not be directly in what you say, but it will be in how you say it. You cannot think, 'This person is an idiot' but say 'I like your thoughtful ideas'. It sounds hypocritical and people see through it straight away. We have to start by changing our thoughts, just as, when faced with rising feelings of hostility, John changed his attitude towards his insurance colleagues.

To change your thoughts, think of the other person in a different way, creating pictures in your mind of them in stages of their life. Think of them first as a baby, dependent on their mother for life. Think of them running around as a toddler. Then picture them progressing through school, with the excitement of learning and the problems of teenage years. Picture them married, and then at home with their family, in an atmosphere of warmth and love. With these pictures in your mind, pick up the phone or drop around to discuss the issue that concerns you. How your communication will change! You will be calm, friendly and sharing a concern. There is less chance for conflict and hostility to arise.

We can be the cause of our own failure. Ben ran a medium-size business in a regional centre, bringing in farm equipment and fuel. He had built it to a nice level and his family lifestyle was terrific. I had helped him get his photo in the local media on several occasions, and wrote a few speeches for him for local groups, such as Rotary. He had a rebellious style, which made him an interesting and entertaining speaker. You can picture Ben: he always wore jeans and boots; had a big gut from too many lunches and too much booze; hated bankers; thought accountants were just bean counters and that teachers should 'get a real job'; and was florid of face, quick to smile and loud to laugh.

But there was another side: Ben was famous for his temper and aggression. In fact, he was proud of it. At lunch, friends would say 'I never want to get on the wrong side of you, Ben' and he would beam. Ben had built something from nothing, and his aggression and hostility had got him to a level of success. But it did not last.

Customers and suppliers became tired of his constant heckling and bad moods. He was fun for a short time but a headache in the long term.

Staff left because Ben had to power over everyone. Customers found alternatives because they wanted a quieter life. As the business declined, Ben became more and more aggressive, and so the decline speeded up. He was communicating anger, hatred and a false sense of what was real. He caused his own failure through reliance on conflict.

LESSONS FROM CHIEF EXECUTIVES

The best way to reduce conflict is to observe how good corporations deal with it—and to learn that, above all, they try to avoid it, seeing conflict as a diversion from the main game. Take a leaf from the corporate book: before any conflict arises, convince yourself that arguing and fighting is not going to bring you or the other person happiness. Unless you believe this, you will be misled into arguments because you have the mistaken view that this form of negative communication will help you get what you want. I've never seen that happen. So, if you think it is going to be useless, maybe even harmful, you will be less likely to respond to conflict with conflict. I've seen some really switched-on chief executives move into action when their company was facing a conflict, including meeting with opposing executives (many of whom they did not even like) and trying every communication angle to resolve the issue so both sides could move on. Interestingly, most of these chief executives began the discussion by acknowledging the real prospect of conflict and the mutual damage this could cause. It's a good reminder for our personal lives.

> *Pretending conflict does not exist... will only make things worse.*

You may hate conflict, but it is inevitable in community groups, sporting clubs, teenage clubs and workplaces. They all operate in a time-stressed environment and interpersonal conflicts happen. The key to moving forward is to deal with these conflicts. When their company faces a conflict, the best chief executives take action straight away. Pretending conflict does not exist, or avoiding dealing with it because you find conflict distasteful, will only make things worse. If you use the right tactics, you can make a real contribution to reducing conflict in any group.

The following tactics have been developed from my observations of how the best chief executives react to forthcoming conflicts.

Look below the surface

An important first tactic is to explore the possibility that there are some deep problems within the group. Of course, you may find that the person creating the conflict is simply a nuisance, but it is wise to consider first whether there is a genuine group problem that needs to be addressed.

Avoid tit for tat reactions

Often this kind of reaction gives the person the response they really wanted, but not necessarily the one that reduces conflict. The Harvard Business School has identified this tit for tat problem and offers some sound advice:

> *One of the most common mistakes managers make is to respond in kind to disruptive behaviour in teams. If Fred explodes at a co-worker, it's tempting to yell back at him, 'Settle down!'. But this reaction only escalates the problem. Moreover, it reinforces Fred's behaviour—he got the reaction he wanted. Instead, try to respond in an unexpected way: change the subject, the tone, or the direction of the meeting. You'll throw Fred off balance and lessen the likelihood that he'll try his tactic again. You may also acknowledge the underlying anger—calmly—and request a change in behaviour. 'I see you're very upset about this, Fred, but I think we could deal with the issue better if you would calm down. Please, sit down, stop pounding the table, and settle down.'*
> Harvard Management Communication Letter, vol. 3, no.4

They are talking about managers, but their advice applies as well for community groups as it does for business.

Don't force an end to conflict

It's tempting for leaders to use their authority to force a solution when conflict arises. This may have short-term impact but, for long-term resolution of group conflict, let the group work on the conflict. They need to go back to the group's goals and objectives and see for themselves that the conflict does not fit.

Don't crush people today; it can ruin them for tomorrow

If one person is playing up, simply crushing them may end the misbehaviour today, but the cost could be that the person leaves the group or makes a lesser contribution to the team. This can be quite a loss, so hesitate and think before you use heavy criticism to end conflict.

ASSERTING YOURSELF IN THE RIGHT WAY

There are some tricky emotional situations when you have to assert yourself. You may find yourself saying 'Yes' instead of 'No', simply to avoid a conflict or confrontation. It is hard to be firm in saying 'No'. Many of the best executives I have worked with shared this problem. Being positive people, they found it difficult to firmly say 'No' when it was needed. Too many finished up saying 'Yes' to some committee recommendation that they knew would waste time and money. I've even worked with one who was so worried about the stability of his personal assistant that he did all his own clerical work rather than delegate it, because delegation risked the hot-tempered assistant making a fuss.

What can you do to be more assertive, while not creating conflict?

Identify your strengths and weaknesses

In a work situation, you will be better able to assert yourself if you have a clear picture of your strengths and weaknesses. You can apply this thinking to the home, a club or the school. If you know what you do best, you will be ready to say 'No' to requests for you to do something that is actually a weakness. You can explain how you make the better contribution, so the other person understands that your 'No' is not personal, but is merely based on how you can work or operate best.

Decide to be strong when needed

You will say 'No' and mean it more often if you have made a prior decision to be strong, not to have everything dumped on you just because you always say 'Yes'. In fact, if you have been overloaded, it's good to let your colleagues, friends or family know that this is the case and that you will be changing things from now on. That way, they are more prepared for you saying 'No' and more likely to understand.

Focus on the bigger picture

Instead of worrying about the feelings of others or talking about yourself when you say 'No' in a business environment, it is good to put the decision in context. 'No, I am unable to do that because my section's priority has been XYZ and we are already behind our schedule.' You can't please everybody, but you can ensure they know why you have taken that decision.

Start with 'no'

The best way to assert yourself is straightaway. So make 'no' the first word you say. Don't ramble or waffle because that just gives you or them time to change your mind. Of course, follow your 'No' with a brief explanation of why. Never make 'no' the only word, because people will then be left to make their own interpretations of your response. Always explain, but not in a lengthy way.

Maintain eye contact

Try to keep a steady, friendly gaze into the other person's or the group's eyes. If you look at the ceiling, cover your mouth or look anxiously back and forth, you will be misunderstood. It's the same if we blurt out 'No' instead of saying it in a friendly and calm manner. One way is convincing and balanced; the other suggests nervousness and lack of control. You like to look at people when you say 'Yes', so be sure you do when you have to say 'No'.

Be open to feedback

Feedback is vital when you are asserting yourself. Don't fall for the 'I will assert myself so I don't need to worry what the other person thinks' line, because that is not true assertiveness. It is something like bullying, but it is not calm self-assertion. Take the opportunity to experience feedback when you say 'no'. If the other person is responding, that is a positive. If you have explained why you said 'No', look for whether the two of you can comfortably move forward and if it is a shared experience. That is, do they understand where you are coming from, even if in the short term they don't like it? If the feedback is all negative (alienating, silence, leading nowhere) then it is time for you to re-evaluate the communication. If the cost of asserting yourself is that people's feedback is always negative, then you are creating the seeds of conflict and not moving forward. The assertiveness will cost you later. Positive assertiveness does not create the ground for later conflict. It deals with the issue of the moment, allowing both sides to move on.

> **Take the opportunity to experience feedback when you say 'no'.**

There are people who specialise in training you to build the skills to handle conflict at work, home or in the community. These courses are generally good. But I have found some of the simplest of techniques and a happy frame of mind prepare people to rid conflict and hostility from their lives.

GAINING INFLUENCE THROUGH COMMUNICATION 18

THE ART OF NEGOTIATION

It's a shame negotiation skills are not taught in school. Most of us feel we would be happier if we could negotiate better. We would certainly achieve earlier promotion if our negotiating skills were excellent. Our lack of skills leaves us feeling unsatisfied and unable to get what we want. Negotiation is a double-edged sword: if we negotiate well, both sides are winners; if we negotiate badly, often both sides are losers. Nobody advances as a result of poor negotiating.

Communication is central to successful negotiating. Indeed, the art of negotiation brings into even sharper focus the truth of: 'Fear is the road to failure; communication is the highway to success'.

Tips for better negotiation

My tips for negotiating are drawn from my corporate communication experience, but also from Rogen International, who are experts in the field. Rogen, among other things, helped Sydney win the Olympic Games for 2000. Their client list and advice are inspirational.

Here are my five tips for better negotiating:

- calmness
- separateness
- giving
- listening
- wrap it up.

Before you start on any of these, develop an attitude of warmth and friendship towards the other person or other party. It is worth doing some mental gymnastics before you begin: think positive thoughts about the other person, feel genuine liking and friendship, and deep concern for their welfare. Ironically, all these make you a better negotiator. This advice will not work if all you want is to be a winner. Negotiation is not going to make you an outright winner. Successful negotiation makes you both winners, so start with a caring approach to the other person. If, on the other hand, you aspire to be the tough leader who wins every time, keep going the way you are. You'll have some early wins in battle, but lose the war. If you want to succeed more often at work, home, school, sport or in the community, learning negotiating skills will help you and those with whom you come in contact.

Calmness

Staying calm is the key to effective communication and is central in good negotiating. By staying calm, you allow the other person to display emotion and say some tough things. You can even acknowledge these without getting angry yourself. This allows you to deal with insults, threats, cynicism or offensive remarks or gestures. Another product of calmness is that, although you will expect your ego and their ego to be playing a part, you won't be a puppet of your ego. Calmness is mutually beneficial and is a good friend in any communication, especially negotiating.

Separateness

If you expect the negotiation to be fairly tough, Rogen International suggest a preliminary discussion to get to know each other's position better, free from any bargaining. This is a great idea, and you can start it by saying, 'I know we have to sort out XYZ soon (suggest a time), but what about a short chat around the subject before we start?' Most people would respond well to this friendly offer. Separateness is like a comfort zone, and you can extend it to a separate brainstorming session if this is helpful. This way, you have both advanced in understanding before the real negotiating begins.

> **Successful negotiation makes you both winners . . .**

Giving

Communication is more about giving than receiving. The irony is, the more you give in communication, the more you receive. It is the same in negotiating. It never hurts to concede the obvious when you are wrong, and, in fact, this is a sign of your goodwill and strength of character. You can extend this to acknowledging another's good points and giving praise when due. This will also prevent you from being negative or from backbiting, both of which produce negative outcomes.

Listening

By asking questions you will become a better listener, and all good negotiators are good listeners too. It is remarkable how often listening plays a key role in communication. In negotiation, it is essential to listen without interrupting. It can be difficult to remain silent in the face of factual errors, but it is better to address these later and respect the right of the other person to put their case without interruption. A colleague of mine had a standard phrase 'Can I just interrupt you there?' and he was generally regarded as a poor communicator.

Wrap it up
Negotiation is not easy, so make sure you don't have to go through it all again and again. Wrap up the negotiation when it is finished: not too early and definitely not too late because things can quickly go off the rails. How do you wrap it up? Summarise important points as you go, and at the end of the meeting agree on a summary of what has been decided and what are the next steps. This may sound too neat and tidy for your personal life, but it is one corporate secret you would do well to apply. Otherwise, your personal life is preoccupied with going over the same things again and again. Ultimately, this satisfies nobody. We would prefer to accept changes, deal with them, negotiate a way forward and move on.

The basis for success

You can see communication at work in negotiation. It quickly exposes those who are stuck in negative communication, and rewards those in the positive. How you are thinking will influence your ability to get what you want. If you find your thoughts are all over the place, you lack confidence, are fearful and closed and starting to imagine things about the other side, then it is time to think again. You will never achieve the calmness or clarity for negotiation while the monkey mind is in charge. Strive for a mind where your thoughts are controlled and you feel self-assured, open and friendly and see things as they really are. This is a great start for effective communication.

> **How you are thinking will influence your ability to get what you want.**

With this presence of mind, your messages can become sharp and clear, honest and simple. They should be something you can consistently repeat and, thinking about who you are negotiating with, they should be able to hit the mark. Anything less will let you down.

Happiness becomes pivotal in negotiation. I have seen this time and again in the corporate world. You will be a poor negotiator if you are desperate for a change. If people can't understand you, how can they help you? If you are self-centred, you finish up letting yourself down, and if you feel as if you always miss out, you most certainly will. Happiness, or lack of it, can make or break negotiations. The best negotiators that I have worked with at corporate level have a confident

> **Happiness, or lack of it, can make or break negotiations.**

feeling that they have what they want and that people understand them. They think of others and have a sense of serenity through their achievements so far. Their happiness provides the perfect platform for successful negotiations.

In a failed negotiation, feedback has often been missing or has been alienating and unsatisfying. The negotiation has led nowhere and has been one-sided. This is a lose-lose situation and people are unlikely to want to negotiate with you again. In a win-win negotiation, the talks have been satisfactory for you and the other side, everybody has been responsive and you can all move forward from this shared experience.

In the art of negotiation, success breeds success, for every good negotiation paves the way for the next.

COMMUNICATING FOR INFLUENCE, NOT FOR CONTROL OR POWER

The best corporations and individuals are not obsessed with having power over other businesses or over people. This has changed modern negotiation, from an act seeking to control to one seeking to influence. Today, corporations are acknowledging the importance of partnerships and of shared success. You will become more influential if you recognise this fact, replacing a drive for more power with a desire for working partnerships. Corporations now recognise that they have little power. On the other hand, they use communication as one way to increase their influence over others.

> ... corporations are acknowledging the importance of partnerships and of shared success.

There is an important distinction between power and influence.

I have found that chief executives and organisations obsessed with power over others are actually small and narrow thinkers, limited by their own imaginations. Even when they think they have control, it turns out to be an illusion. Rarely are their companies good places to work; few people report them as happy workplaces.

On the other hand, those leaders who are open to other people, who can flow with them and with situations, create an immense influence on the way things turn out. These leaders bring out the best in people and organisations, based on teamwork and partnership. Control is about making one person happy at the expense of another; influence is about making both people happy.

The difference between control and influence may seem subtle at first, but it is worth studying because by leaning towards influence you will become a better communicator. You may also become a better person.

Think of it this way: those who want control see you and me as completely different beings who will compete, and only one of us can win. You probably know people who operate this way. Generally, these people are afraid that unless they get control, they won't get what they want. Win everything, or lose the lot, is their attitude. If you are worried that they do not seem to like you very much, don't be; they like themselves even less. They fail to realise that with effective communication they can ask for anything and, by seeking to influence, they have a better chance of getting it.

Think of increasing your communication skills in the same way as playing a guitar. Do you have control over the guitar? No, because there are certain things it can do and certain things you can't. However, the more skills you have, the more influence you have over the sounds the guitar makes. It's the same with communication.

There's nothing wrong with influence. Almost all good outcomes are the result of an intermingling of different influences that, often enough, give rise to an outcome greater than the sum of the inputs.

If you are obsessed with control you are likely to lose patience with communication: 'I can't get exactly what I want. People are too slow for me. Why don't they see my point of view?'. These then become reasons, in your control-dominated mind, not to bother with effective communication any more, but to go for even more control in the first place. Does this sound like anyone you know?

People who prefer to influence others and events, using effective communication as a major tool, tend to have more respect for others and appear happier. People like their company and seek it out, thereby increasing their influence.

In summary, when it comes to using communication to have power over other organisations or other people, you will find it rarely works. As for communicating to create influence or make an impact, you can have all you want.

IMPACT NOT POWER

The Gallup Organisation has developed the StrengthsFinder system, identifying a person's life themes—recurring patterns of thought, feeling or behavior. The more dominant a life theme is in a person, the greater the impact it will have on their behaviour and performance. The life themes are grouped into four major types: relating, impacting, striving and thinking.

The impacting type can be useful for those of you still grappling with the difference between influence and power. You want impact, but there is an alternative way of looking at impact other than the traditional way of having power over others. Gallup found that people who were strong in impact had the following qualities:

- **Command.** You want to be in charge, and you are often the person that others expect to make decisions.
- **Competition.** You measure your progress against the performance of others. You strive to win first place and revel in contests.
- **Developer.** You recognise and cultivate the potential in others. You spot the signs of each small improvement and derive satisfaction from these.
- **Maximiser.** You focus on strengths as a way to stimulate personal and group excellence. You seek to transform something strong into something superb.
- **Positivity.** Your enthusiasm is contagious. You are upbeat and can get others excited about what they are doing.
- **Woo.** You love the challenge of meeting new people and winning them over. You derive satisfaction from breaking the ice and making connection.

Does this sound like you? If so, you are lucky, and already on the way to achievement, without the distraction of a neurotic focus on power over people. Of course, those of you who relate most to having impact should constantly be aware of the danger of going after power for power's sake, whether as a person, a company or a community group. Impact is not the same as power. Communication plays a key role for those who have an impact; they are aware of other people and can improve and motivate them, through communication.

BECOME A 'RELATING' TYPE

Another of the life themes identified by the Gallup Organisation's StrengthsFinder system is 'relating', and this is one that could really help you overcome failure and fear. If you can build up the relating side of yourself, communication will become a pathway to greater success and personal happiness. This applies to individuals, corporations and community groups. Within the relating type there are several characteristics, and Gallup's description of them provides a good base for self-evaluation:

- **Communication.** You generally find it easy to put your thoughts into words, are a good conversationalist and would make a good presenter.
- **Empathy.** You sense the feelings of other people by imagining yourself in others' lives or situations.
- **Harmony.** You look for consensus. You don't enjoy conflict, and instead seek areas of agreement.
- **Inclusiveness.** You are accepting of others. You show awareness of those who feel left out and make an effort to include them.

- **Individualisation.** You are intrigued with the unique qualities of each person. You have a gift for figuring out how people who are different from each other can work together productively.
- **Relator.** You enjoy close relationships, finding deep satisfaction in working hard with friends to achieve a goal.
- **Responsibility.** You take psychological ownership of what you say and do. You are committed to stable values, such as honesty and loyalty.

Wouldn't it be good if everybody developed these characteristics? These themes should be on your office wall, on the fridge door at home and corporate meeting rooms as a constant reminder of the positive way to behave. These values and attributes are not wishy-washy or weak. Rather, they can be the foundation of success and prosperity. We would all like to live and work with someone like this. A good start is to become someone like this ourselves.

The empathy theme strikes a strong note, because this can help you arrive at greater balance and perspective. Through empathy, you will not be envious of the success of others, or overly critical of those who do not quite make it. You will be more likely see things and people as they really are, instead of being dominated by the illusions created through fear.

PART 4

Presenting and selling

19 Successful presentations 135
20 Make meetings work for you 140
21 Surviving parties 146
22 Secrets of a good speech 150
23 Is the customer always right? 159
24 Think of the future as e-life 167

SUCCESSFUL PRESENTATIONS

AVOID THE 'ME, ME, ME' APPROACH

'Just a little background on us.' These six words can strike boredom into the hearts of executives around the boardroom table as some hopeful supplier begins a presentation with their greatest obsession: themselves. These words are an informal signal to everybody to switch off, and wait for the real message later. Self-obsession can hold back your career and your personal life by alienating bosses and driving friends and loved ones away. It can stall your career, just when you face the opportunity for success. So, learn from how corporate presentations go wrong.

Often, after saying they will provide 'just a little background on us', the presenters show their company hierarchy, office or plant locations, logos and brand images, clients or customers, and profit performance, and they go on and on. The presenters are so interested in themselves that they don't notice the audience quietly nodding off, or doodling on their notepads. What is wrong with this? What can you learn from it?

What is wrong is that the presentation is self-absorbed, possibly arrogant and does not focus on the target audience. By nature, we view things from our own perspective, so we want to know what all this means for us, and how you can help us. If you talk too much and too often about yourself, you are making the same mistake. Although people may smile and nod as you talk, they will be bored. Most would feel it is rude to say so, so you never get to find out that you have been a real bore.

It is not that giving information about yourself is wrong. In fact, it is important to communicate about yourself. The mistake lies in doing it at the expense of meaning and feedback. There is a time and place for everything in communication. For example, the time to discuss your global locations is when you are telling board members that their job needs a supplier with feet on the ground in key global markets. Here it is relevant and adds to understanding. But if the presenter is proudly listing global locations out of context, that is with no reference to the listener, then it becomes boring.

In PR and marketing, effective communication about yourself is called 'stressing the benefits' of what you have, rather than the features. The benefits only make sense in the context of what the client wants, so most of your communication begins with that, and only moves to yourself when relevant. In successful business presentations, the speaker spends most of the time talking about the audience. This is far more appealing than talking about their own company. People are fascinated to hear somebody talking about their operation, and flattered when the speaker has done their homework. This could work well for you in your personal and business relationships. Think of others first, yourself second or last. Applying this business secret builds the basis for good personal communication.

BURST THROUGH THE BRIEF

One of the most successful business pitch advisers is a firm called Rogen International. They use the expression 'burst through the brief'. Organisations that win competitive pitches tend to be those who do not accept the brief as rigid, who see it as a starting point and look for an angle or an add-on that will deliver more value. This is a little like thinking outside the square and adds a heightened interest through unpredictability. Many business briefs are poorly written, often not revealing what the company really wants. Rogen advise clients to dig deeper, find out what the prospect really wants and then deliver it. It's much the same in our daily lives. When people express things poorly to us, the best communicators are those who probe further to find out what the person is really on about. Listening and asking questions become good allies in successful communication.

> *Think of others first, yourself second or last.*

LEARN FROM THE BEST BUSINESS PRESENTATIONS

Apply your knowledge of corporate communication to business presentations, for it works as strongly there as anywhere else. Being well prepared is the starting point and, instead of letting your thoughts roam all over the place, try to have them under control as you present. Feel self-assured and be open and friendly towards the people in the room. If you show a lack of confidence and are closed off, you will quickly lose their attention. With this frame of mind, your messages can be more effective, so long as you give them a sharp focus and clarity. Avoid talking in riddles or using jargon. Instead, speak in an honest and simple way, repeating key messages as you go. In this way, you will hit the mark.

> *Feel self-assured and be open and friendly towards the people in the room.*

Happiness is a factor in business presentations. I have worked with presentation teams who are having great fun, and they win the business. I have also worked with presentation teams where tension is high; they miss out. A happy approach means you feel fairly content with yourself (confident), which allows you to consider others. People will think that it may be fun to work with you.

To be truly good at business presentations, you will need to develop a strong antenna for feedback. Be aware when people are being responsive, make it feel like a shared experience and, where relevant, encourage them to comment. This will ensure that the exchange is satisfying to you and to them. If, on the other hand, there are no responses and the audience appears closed off, take a bit of a risk and ask them what their main concerns are at this point. You can then build the remainder of your presentation within those concerns.

Here are some more tips on good business presentations.

Start out strong

I've heard it said that speakers have up to eight seconds initially to capture the audience's attention or lose them forever. This is a bit overstated for me, but it does highlight the need to start with a bang. That's why a beginning like 'Just a few words about us' leaves people cold. Instead, arouse their interest and involvement by starting your presentation with a question. The moment that people detect a question coming, they are attentive. Or start by summing up the whole thing in a surprisingly short number of words: 'In the next ten minutes we will outline three ways you are currently losing money, and five reasons why our system can add to your bottom line'. That will get most of them listening. Having started well, you have to deliver the goods.

Believe your own message

An oft repeated regret of politicians is that you can't fake sincerity, and this is also true of passion and emotion. You can't fake a passionate belief in what you are saying. Yet often it is passion that causes one side to win over another. If we see a presenter who obviously believes in their product or service, we choose them over one who is just going through the presentation like a robot. We admire human commitment and that comes from how you feel.

Look them in the eye

One of the most powerful tools in a business presentation is using your eyes. Eye contact is the best way to link yourself with the audience. The reverse is also true; avoid eye contact and you create a separation between you and the audience. Creating a positive link with the audience is the most critical reason for eye contact, though it is also said to add to your sincerity.

> *Eye contact is the best way to link yourself with the audience.*

To be able to look at your audience, you will need to know your presentation well. There are times when you may need to read from some text or refer to notes. This is okay as long as it does not last for a long time. Turn to the notes completely, read them and then turn your gaze back to the audience. A prolonged break from eye contact generally means most of the audience will stop looking at you, meaning they concentrate less on what you're saying and more on what they're thinking. That's bad for your presentation.

Wrap up well

To finish, you just need to sum things up. But many presenters allow things to fizzle out, making them look as if they've run out of ideas. It is best to leave your audience knowing that there is so much more for you to say but you want to get on with their comments. Too often this summary is overlooked, is too long or misses the point. Go back to where you started, and repeat the promise you made in the introduction. One leading speaker says the best speeches tell the audience what they are about to hear, tell them, then finish by telling them what they just heard. Good conclusions warn the audience that you are about to finish; and then they tell the audience what it is that you want them to do. Never leave the audience wondering. If you are there to ask for their support or their contract, summarise why they should choose you and finish by asking for it. Subtlety rarely works, so finish with the key point you want to get across.

> **Never leave the audience wondering.**

Concluding well is vital to successful business presentations. Yet many presenters overlook this part. 'Oh, then I'll just wrap things up' is what they say during rehearsals, and this makes me very nervous. Treat the conclusion as the most important part of your presentation and you will leave time for it, you will prepare for it and you will deliver it well. Without planning, your conclusion will be waffle. Worse, your unprepared conclusion creates a climate of confusion around everything that has gone before, leaving audiences wondering what it was all about. It's no fun for them to be left this way. They want and need guidance, and a good conclusion provides this. It tells them what to do next. But keep the conclusion short and to the point. At that stage, they are ready for you to close, so do it well and briefly.

Our best corporations have learned from experience that good presentations need preparation. They make sure there is time for their executives to be prepared for the important pitch. Most of this preparation focuses on who they are pitching to. The core of preparation should be a description of what the audience needs and how you will provide that need. That's why phrases such as 'Just a few words about us' have no place in good presentations.

20 MAKE MEETINGS WORK FOR YOU

As a young person I had a secret terror of meetings. Meetings were, in my mind, an opportunity for the superstars to shine and for ordinary, shy people like me to be ignored or humiliated. This is a pretty extreme view (or is it?), but many people suffer from some degree of fear of meetings. One of the outcomes is that when they do have a positive contribution to make, they speak with so little confidence that the meeting almost ignores their point. Good points poorly expressed are almost as bad as having nothing to say. For me, meetings were just occasions when the heat of the spotlight could be on me and embarrassment would follow. With the value of experience and hindsight, I now see this as a self-centred view of meetings. Again, many of us have this view.

> **Good points poorly expressed are almost as bad as having nothing to say.**

Have you been to team meetings at work and hated it? Management holds the meeting with the aim of creating a good feeling, a real team buzz and a positive piece of communication. Too many of these meetings leave people feeling uneasy, even threatened. Instead of building communication and involvement, they become opportunities for a few to grandstand and for most of us to feel ill at ease, bored or in the wrong place at the wrong time. You can learn from these management mistakes, so that you drive for clarity and purpose in any meeting you attend.

Many of you will have been to meetings at the local sporting club, school or community group, and come away totally confused or frustrated. There are probably more bad meetings than good ones. Yet meetings are one way for modern people to communicate, so it is wise to make them work for you.

WHAT MAKES BAD MEETINGS SO BAD?

Management, sporting club or team meetings are generally ruined at the beginning, because they start out with no clear purpose. It is not enough that the boss or someone else feels there is a need to give everyone a bit of motivation. This kind of objective is too general and invites disaster when the meeting heads off the topic. Bad meetings do not start or finish on time. People make a special effort to be there at the appointed time, and gradually lose their sense of goodwill as they wait for the rest, including the boss, to turn up. As the meeting goes over time, people become fidgety and anxious. To make bad meetings worse, the meeting leader has no idea who should be there and therefore has to ask 'Is everybody here?' Of course, this same leader has not bothered to check the room, so on arrival the lights are off and it soon becomes obvious the airconditioning is not working, the AV gear is not plugged in and there is no whiteboard.

Any or all of the above meeting faults happen at work every day. They also happen at the local school, in sporting clubs, charities and local community group meetings. Some places claim these faults as part of their culture. Some colleagues estimate that bad meetings with negative results outweigh the good ones by five to one. It's enough to put you off the concept of meetings as a communication technique.

THE BEST APPROACH TO MEETINGS

Of the hundreds of corporate meetings I have attended, the best performers at meetings were those who gave the meeting clear and sharp messages. Everybody knew what they stood for and what they wanted. If you want to perform better and achieve more at meetings, focus especially on the clarity of your messages. The best corporate executives have this area right under control. I've seen some poor corporate performers too, sadly some of these in senior positions. Their messages at meetings were confused or confusing. There are even cases of straightforward deceit, which are always found out, eventually. These failing executives were inconsistent and nobody was ever sure what or who it was all for.

> ... focus especially on the clarity of your messages.

The best corporate executives have a really positive attitude to meetings. After the small talk and the smiles, they would quickly deliver their message with focus and clarity, coming across in an honest and simple way. They would find opportunities in the meeting to repeat their messages, perhaps using slightly different language, and always made sure their messages hit the mark. I have seen the best executives even delay the closure of a meeting, just as everybody is about to rush off, in order to make sure there is clarity on what has been decided and where everyone should go from here. 'I know we are all under pressure and want to get to some urgent business elsewhere, but we will have wasted a lot of time here today if we are not all clear on where we go from here. Are we all clear that . . . ?' is their style of communication. This brings people back to the core points and bonds them to the way forward.

People tend to love what they create. As much as anything else, this underpins the value of good meetings. Outstandingly positive results can be achieved in meetings, so it is worth trying until you get it right. For a start, if you are responsible for a meeting, be prepared and lead people towards the core purpose. Be gracious when people get off the topic. Be friendly to all, and thank them for their participation.

The communication technique of asking for questions can be one of your most valued allies as you strive to make a meeting work. When you ask for questions, always do so with a smile and even a nod of your head, to show you mean it. Some go as far as holding up their hand as they invite questions, physically showing people what to do. It helps to be specific about what the questions should cover and, when someone does ask a question, as meeting leader you should look and listen with total focus.

As in most communication, it helps meetings if you are grateful for contributions, so remember to thank people when they make a comment or ask a question. On the other hand, if someone is making a hostile point, handle it with the utmost cordiality, because this will take the heat out of the issue and allow you to get on with business. If someone is particularly strong with their hostility, perhaps you could deflect it by asking the group to contribute on the topic, and ask specifically if anyone else has had the same feelings or treatment.

> **Do anything to avoid an angry response . . .**

If you find yourself getting annoyed by what others are saying, count to three before you respond. If necessary, count to one hundred. Do anything to avoid an angry response, because anger will only be the cause of your own downfall. Some people seem to get caught on the hook of anger, and spend their whole life in a highly disturbed state, alienating others. This communicates failure and frustration. If, on the other hand, you are able to confront both great hostility and great praise with a neutral perspective, bringing everyone back to the topic at hand, you will communicate effectiveness, success, confidence and purpose. People will be grateful and the job will be done in a happier environment.

The way you close a meeting is critical to the success of it in terms of communication. We tend to remember best what we hear last. Hence, if you are in charge of a meeting, always finish with a friendly summary of what it was about, the key points to emerge and the next action to be taken. This helps everyone leave on a good note and, more importantly, with a clear idea of what they have just been doing.

'I LOVE MEETINGS, REALLY I DO'

Here is my 'I love meetings, really I do' strategy.

Find out what it's about

Before the meeting, get a clear picture of the purpose of the meeting. It may be to set new budgets, plan the wedding of your child, manage the next soccer season or organise the school fete. If you know the central purpose, you will be less likely to be diverted by the inevitable side issues. In fact, you will be able to help the group get back on track. It also enables you to come along prepared, having gathered some essential facts or information to help.

Set your own objectives

Knowing what the meeting is for, decide what your own goals are at that meeting. What points do you need to make, what do you want people to think of you, what decisions would you like? That is, know your own mind. If you have a solution to a problem, present it as an option rather than as a non-negotiable total solution.

Listen

Listening is essential to all communication. If you prepare by knowing what the meeting is for, assembling some essential information and working out what you want, you will be better able to listen to others. You may even be able to cultivate an open mind, particularly if you remind yourself that everyone around the table is likeable and, just like you, is in search of happiness.

Make a contribution

People who turn up at meetings and never, or only rarely, make a contribution are seen by others as oddballs or outsiders. Put your information on the table, but keep it open so the group can reject part of it without taking you head on. At the same time, take a genuine interest in the points others are making. If you are lost for words, ask a question or seek clarification from someone about an earlier point. It gets you into the loop.

Smile inside and out

At meetings you have to keep your cool. Be nice to people who are making stupid points, smile at weak jokes and take criticism on the chin even if it is nonsense. If this sounds insincere, remind yourself that while you must be sincere and share your feelings in intimate, important personal relationships, when it comes to group meetings the reverse can often be the case. This is a group dynamic that you cannot control, but you can influence it by being well prepared and determined to be friendly at all times.

SOME FURTHER SUGGESTIONS

Some of our most persuasive corporate leaders use some pretty simple techniques to guide meetings to a successful conclusion. Brian, a senior partner in a business consultancy firm, told me meetings dominate his whole day. As he said, 'I start off at 8 a.m. with a team meeting, head off to my first client meeting at 9 and spend the rest of the day racing from one meeting to another.' I expressed horror at the pattern of his day, and asked him how he could possibly keep focus in this kind of rush. He produced a small card from his pocket, with the following words:

- emotional connection
- common ground
- objectives, objectives, objectives
- shared agendas.

These words were his meetings mantra, and he looked at the card at virtually every meeting. This created the real value of his contribution, making him worth the fortune his clients were paying. Brian put it this way: 'I always try to make an emotional connection with people, even if I have to resort to a motherhood statement. With emotion comes trust and confidence, and I build emotion by speaking with conviction during the meeting'. He said a key was to search out the common ground by listening closely to each point of view. He respected each point of view and tried to see where commonality arose, because he saw common ground as the key to ultimate agreement. He also saw it as his role as a consultant to bring people back to the objectives of the meeting—the 'Why are we here?' question. Brian again: 'Almost every meeting at some stage goes off the rails. Some of them need to stay there for a while, but all of them need to come back to objectives if they are to achieve anything at all. Most meetings that fail do so because there is no agreement on the objectives of the meeting'. Building on this, Brian always has an agenda, a plan of attack, before every meeting and is willing to share this with others. Setting and sharing agendas with others becomes a key step in creating teamwork and building agreement. You can apply his techniques to any meeting, whether at a sporting club, planning for a wedding, at the child-care centre or in local politics. These techniques work for meetings large and small.

> ... search out the common ground by listening closely to each point of view.

Having a technique will reduce your fear of meetings, though it will not remove fear entirely. If, like me, you are suffering from a fear of meetings, you can deal with it logically as a fear arising from self-centredness, or some other irrational cause. But for many it is best to deal with fear emotionally. It can be helpful prior to the meeting to close your eyes and visualise the meeting. In your mind, look on everyone there with warmth and friendship, picture their faces and smile in your mind, and feel good thoughts going out to them. Then bring your mind back to yourself, applying that same feeling of warmth and friendship. Before opening your eyes, tell yourself that you really like everyone who will be there and you really like yourself. Now go to it. What has all this got to do with good communication? If you replace fear with a feeling of warmth, friendship and personal happiness, you will communicate with a smile, you will be open and you will get your message across. Good communication starts by getting rid of that fear.

21 SURVIVING PARTIES

I hate parties. I've finally worked out why. First, there is the panic feeling that I will be standing in the middle of the room, alone, while everyone else is in a group having fun. Second, if I do open a conversation I know it will be with the most boring person in the room and I'll be stuck with them. I know that, for many of you, genuine fear makes social functions a real agony.

If you want to do better, there are some techniques that can help. When I use the term 'party', I mean any social gathering apart from the family Christmas. In these social gatherings, there will be people who are important to you now or in the future: whether this is at work, a conference, school, the child-care centre, a sporting club or a community group. If every time there is a function all you do is grab the arm of a familiar person and talk to nobody else, you're not really using the function for networking. Others, observing your clinging, will put you in a category and perhaps not see your true potential. So there is a lot to gain and a lot to lose at these so-called social functions. My approach? Treat these functions just like work: go to the function, meet lots of people, talk to the important ones (or at least make eye contact and nod a greeting), say hello to your friends and then get out, go home, have fun.

> **So there is a lot to gain and a lot to lose at these so-called social functions.**

Here's a secret about those people who appear to be having such a good, chatty time: many of them were like you a few moments ago, standing on their own. Others have finally found some friends and are too frightened to let them go, so they're talking their heads off and appearing to have fun, and they will stay in that group all night. At parties, looks can be deceiving. Certain people can look to be successful, but all they have managed to do is corner the same people and talk the same talk. How is that improving their network, adding to their promotion chances, bringing spice to their life? It isn't. They're just too scared to succeed in the art of the party. It can take courage to get the most out of parties, because you have to be prepared to leave the security of friends and open up discussion somewhere else.

HOW CAN YOU SURVIVE PARTIES?

The first thing is to realise that they are not really parties. Parties are organised functions where we get a chance to communicate with a wide range of people. Most of this communication could have some bearing on our career, our business, our community standing or our future. That is, a party is like a noisy interview. It's like one hundred auditions all happening at once. It is, above all, a performance, with unwritten rules and pitfalls for the unwary. If you think they are just parties, you may appear like a fool to the manager looking to promote you. See the hidden dangers of parties?

Looking and sounding as if you have something to say, that you are on a mission, is a good way to approach these functions. People will generally take notice of this. For example, 'Hi, Barry. I want to find time to have a chat to you about some of the latest figures we've been developing. Now is not the right time, but will you be in town over the next few weeks?'. This is effective at business functions, because it sounds important. You've given Barry the chance to tell you how busy he is and how much he will be in and out of town, and you seem to have been discussing something important and interesting, while talking about nothing much at all. A further real plus of this approach is that it does open an opportunity for you to follow up with Barry if he is a business target.

> *It is . . . a performance, with unwritten rules and pitfalls for the unwary.*

What if you have made eye contact with someone you don't know? Obviously, the technique above won't work. Instead, try saying 'Did we meet before at one of these functions?'. That is nice and open-ended, and who knows who they met at a social function, so it gives you the chance to explore that option for a while. It's a lot better than the question, 'So, what brings you to this function?'. A bit embarrassing when you get the response, 'Well, actually, I'm the host'.

The next tip for survival at parties is not to stand in one spot if you are on your own. If you stand still, you will feel uncomfortable and left out. The best tip is to meander slowly between the groups, as if you belong there and have a purpose, but not so fast that you can't stop and chat when the chance arises. Make eye contact as you go and, if there is more than a flicker from the other person, you can say 'Hello' and you've just succeeded at meeting a new person. As you meander, try to keep a smile going, because that is a far better conversation starter than a look of panic.

A colleague of mine is expert at seeing a small gap in a group and edging his way in. Eventually, he becomes part of the group. He has to put up with a few awkward moments when he's not quite in the group and not quite out of it, but after those moments he's in. He can start talking to complete strangers as if they are old friends, because they have been sharing this group chat. This technique is not for me, but it may work for you.

Having something prepared that you want to discuss is good. If it's the end-of-year party for your sporting club and you want to encourage junior development, have some thoughts ready on the topic. Then talk to people about how they think the season or the club is going, and pick up their points as an opportunity to introduce your point on the juniors. It gives it a nice flow. But don't put notes in your pocket, because you will worry about them. Instead, put some notes in your mind. Have some questions ready, such as 'Did you see any weaknesses in our approach this season?'. Don't rush into groups, because that gives them the chance to split up and you're on your own again.

Specific comment is better than being too general. For example, 'What's the next six months looking like in your field?' is far more likely to prompt discussion than 'What's the next six months looking like in the economy?'. People will talk most comfortably about themselves, rather than the bigger picture.

Another important 'don't' if you are alone and uncomfortable is don't stand near the bar, whatever you do. The combination is lethal—by the time you do get to talk to someone you will not be making any sense. People who do well at parties have two or three drinks, maximum. Some of the real professionals have soft drink only.

When you are standing alone in the middle of a crowd, don't look at it as rejection, look at it as opportunity. This is really hard to do, but smile anyway.

Before you go to a function, it is a good idea to review where you are, by running through your state of mind, and see whether you are either negative or positive. Follow up by evaluating your messages. Have they been clear lately? Do you have any messages? If not, then before any function or meeting, spend a few minutes deciding on some key things you would like to communicate. Make sure you can express them clearly, that they are honest, simple and more in the positive than the negative.

Mind and messages won't get you far if you are not happy. Unhappiness has a way of shining through. It is a great communicator. Dissatisfaction, for some a way of life, fits in the same category. If, on the other hand, you can review yourself and find that by and large you have what you want, people understand most things about you, you like people and have a sense of achievement, then note these things because it means you are happier than most. It's a good feeling to take along with you. If you're consistently showing up in the negative

> **If you're consistently showing up in the negative ... it is time for a major rethink ...**

(most of us are there sometimes), it is time for a major rethink and maybe some professional help to evaluate where you are and where you could be.

Before you go to that party, remember the importance of feedback. Listen for it, encourage it, ask questions. Think about how feedback has been over the past week, and if it is more negative than positive perhaps it is time to be more open and accepting of messages from other people, and less focused on your own. Thinking about feedback will almost always make you more alert to it and better at encouraging it.

The final tip on parties is to know when enough is enough. Parties can be mentally demanding and there is a point when everything has been said and done. This is the time to move on. Remember, if you view a party as work, it makes a lot of sense to network with as many people as you can in a short time, and then get out of there. If it is all finally too much and there are no real openings, go home. At least you showed up. Isn't showing up at least half of what parties are for?

22 SECRETS OF A GOOD SPEECH

> **Bad speechmaking will hold back your career.**

To learn how to make a really good speech, it helps to know what makes a bad speech. I've heard plenty of bad ones, as corporate presenters fumble their way to obscurity. Bad speechmaking will hold back your career. The worst speeches come from people who do not really like their audience very much, and don't like themselves either. Negative attitudes show up in a speech by the speechmaker taking no account of the audience, generally delivering in a monotone and reflecting badly on themselves. The best speeches come from people who are happy and really interested in communicating with others. This happiness and interest is reflected in a speech of high personal interest to the audience, delivered with some confidence and reflecting well on speaker and audience.

Why bother making good speeches? At many stages in your career, community and social life, speaking will help you get ahead, whether at a school fete, customer briefing, sales conference, team seminar, board meeting, business pitch, university lecture, welfare issue meeting or community function.

SIX WAYS TO RUIN A SPEECH

Beware of these six big ways to ruin a speech.

Badly told jokes

Good jokes badly told are worse than no jokes at all. When in doubt, throw the joke out.

What is the point?

A bad speech never tells us what it is all about. The question grows: 'What is the point?'. This is the last thought we have before nodding off.

Lots of facts

It's impossible to pay attention to a multitude of statistics and facts. We are mere human beings. On the other hand, selectively used facts become a powerful persuader.

Head down, eyes on the page

When the speaker is more focused on the notes than on us, it is easy for our minds to wander. Speaking up, eye contact, voice projection, positive body language, energy and enthusiasm, using your hands and arms—these can all add impact.

On, and on, and on

When a speech is in a monotone, we have no idea what is really important; the speaker's presentation gives us no clues.

All of a sudden, it's over

Just when we were settling into a comfortable coma, the speaker seems to have finished. This is disappointing and awkward: Should we clap now? What was the point again?

OVERCOMING STAGE FRIGHT

One of the biggest barriers to communicating in new work locations or within a changed corporation is stage fright, being scared that you may not be able to cope, or even to talk. Stage fright becomes worse when presenting to a group or making a formal speech. You are not on your own here. Most of us feel this form of fear at some stage, and the most common occurrence is when we're talking with strangers, just when we need to make new friends. Our comfort zone has disappeared; we are truly alone although surrounded by people. Corporate communication training programs provide some of the best solutions to help you overcome stage fright, or at least to help you cope better.

Preparation is essential

Any corporate executive who has to make a speech or presentation to a group of people they have never met knows that the first step is to be prepared. The first thing they do is try to find out more about the audience, what they do, where they are from and what they hope to gain by listening. From there, they prepare their material, becoming totally familiar with the key parts, such as the opening sentences and the conclusion. Preparation, they know, will reduce their anxiety. It seems that when we know what we want to get across, what we are going to say and how we will say it, we become less anxious and less nervous. Mark Twain claimed it took him three weeks to prepare an impromptu, totally off-the-cuff speech.

> *Preparation, they know, will reduce their anxiety.*

151

Here are some tips on preparation. These work for speeches and also work for getting to know new friends.

Know yourself and your topic
Don't ever try to bluff, whether to a large group or to one other person. We all have 'bluff antennas' and can spot it in an instant. We also know an expert, and that is someone who is prepared, knows more than they have time to tell us and is able to listen with confidence to our questions or comments. When you meet new people, it is a mistake to try to create a new you. Be yourself. Despite your monkey mind raising doubts about whether you are interesting, you are, so be comfortable with yourself and others will be comfortable with you.

> ... it is a mistake to try to create a new you.

Memorise the opening lines
The first minute or so of any presentation or speech is the time of greatest anxiety, so you will be more comfortable if you have memorised your introduction. For meeting new friends, you may have a standard way of breaking the ice. Holding out your hand to shake hands and saying, 'Hi, I'm Steve Manallack' isn't a bad start. You may extend to 'I'm new in this office and can't even find the coffee machine ...'. In most cases, you will find people helpful, exchanging names and becoming a recognised face in your new environment.

Focus on them, not you

TV presenters and circuit speechmakers know that the moment their attention shifts from their audience to themselves, they become nervous. By being self-focused, they are hit by stage fright and their performance suffers. The best secret for talking to a group, large or small, is to pick out one or two people and talk to them, smile to them and feed off their responses. You can't apply this to the whole group, but by looking from one person and then across the group to the other person, everyone feels you are talking to them. If you just look across the whole group and smile you may get no response. Instead, pick out one person and smile at them. They will smile back, and so will others. Some professional speakers focus on one person until they get a response, such as a smile or a nod of the head, and then they move on to somebody else and do the same. These are all tricks for keeping your attention out there, and not on yourself.

> ... pick out one or two people and talk to them ...

Greet the sweating

You're about to make that speech or to meet new people. Your heart is beating faster, your palms are sweaty and your legs seem a little weak. Most people feel these physical reactions and their only thought is 'I'm terrified', with the next thought being 'I can't do this'. There is another way of thinking that has helped many corporate executives and it takes some practice. When you feel the heart beating, the sweat starting and the knees wobbling, instead of thinking 'I'm terrified' why not switch to 'I'm excited'? The next thought after 'I'm excited' is 'I'm really on my toes now'. It is a small, subtle difference of thinking that can transform fear to excitement, failure to success.

They say 30 per cent of us would rather die than speak in public. Having sat through some appalling speeches, I can see some merit in this view. But even bad speechmakers can become better. A speech is just another form of human communication, after all. We can all talk. Speaking is an inevitable part of being involved in the community, so it is good to improve this skill. A speech is just talking, but to a larger group.

> *... instead of thinking 'I'm terrified' why not switch to 'I'm excited'?*

Of course, you can't take anything for granted in making speeches, and I was guilty of this when a colleague mentioned to me that he was a bit nervous about making a speech in a few days time. The speech was to over one hundred people. I knew this colleague well, respected his work and had seen him time and again charm our clients and perform well around the boardroom table when there were ten or so people. I took it for granted he could translate these skills to public speaking, so merely assured him his concerns were not worth worrying about, that the speech would be fine. I remained confident as he went to the podium to begin the speech. But as he began to talk, I was gripped by a real concern that I had let him down. You see, making this speech to over one hundred people, my colleague had changed from a confident, friendly communicator to one dominated by fear. His voice had changed: it was thin and it lacked persuasion. I noticed the vigorous shaking of his hands, the rapid movement of his eyes and the shuffling of his feet. His voice also shook, so that the entire audience knew this was a painfully fearful experience for him. Instead of listening to what he was saying, they forgot the message and were concerned about his fear and whether he could even finish the speech.

Here was one person who could grab a small audience in the palm of his hand, but could not face a large audience. For him (and for the audience) it was a painful experience, and one he should not have gone through, because fear can be largely overcome, or at least transformed into a more positive emotion. I made a mental note to recommend him to a speech trainer when the next opportunity arose.

THINKING ABOUT THE AUDIENCE

Like most things in successful communication, a good speech starts with thinking and planning, particularly thinking about who your audience is. If you like people, you will try to give them what they want.

Do you remember how good Muhammed Ali was at his peak? 'Float like a butterfly, sting like a bee' must be one of the most powerful metaphors of all time. So much better than a boxer sitting in a media conference discussing the virtues of his foot movement, his extra speed, the power of his jab and so on. 'Float like a butterfly, sting like a bee' was Ali. It was all we needed to know about his technique, and his personality. Ali also liked to use the power of the rhythm, another effective way of making a potentially dull speech much more exciting.

Why do we use metaphors? We use them because they are so easily understood. They capture the big idea in a few words. On top of that, the metaphor seems to make things relevant, as if it rings a relevance button in the brain of the audience.

To put it simply, a good speech or presentation must go beyond the intellectual and the words—it must touch people emotionally. As a speaker you need to consider how you want your listeners to feel about what you are saying. Unless you are clear on this, your speech will become dull. Your listeners won't form any emotional response, so most of it will just go over their heads.

As you prepare a speech, instead of thinking about yourself or your special subject, think about the people who will be listening. From there on, it is easier to avoid the six ways to ruin a speech.

A good friend of mine, Malcolm Gray, has made a career in TV, radio and public speaking, now spending much of his time training people in the art. One of the most valuable tips from his book *Public Speaking* (BRW Business Library, Information Australia, 1999) is to start each speech by preparing a purpose sentence, for example, 'The purpose of this speech is to (persuade/inform/move) my target audience with the thought that . . .'.

While Malcolm suggests using this to underpin your speech preparation, you could also use it fairly early in your introduction, so the audience knows what's coming. Note that he thinks there are three types of speech: persuasive, informative and emotional. A persuasive speech says, 'Here are the benefits to you personally'. An informative speech says, 'Here are the facts'. An emotive speech says, 'Let me massage your feelings'. Some speeches contain elements of all three.

I've trained a lot of corporate executives, professional firm partners and others in speechmaking. Because I am not a professional speech trainer, I keep my advice pretty simple, leaving them with six key points:

- Always prepare a speech—never speak off the cuff unless you have to.

- Keep in the front of your mind that you really like these people.
- Plan a speech that is shorter than the allotted time—the audience enjoys brevity.
- Don't tell jokes, but do have some humour at your own expense.
- Tell the audience what is coming—it increases anticipation.
- Sum up what you said, so they'll remember it.

You might be making a speech at a friend's birthday, talking at the local community centre or presenting to a group of people who will control your career. The first step is always the same: prepare.

Ninety per cent of people who speak off the cuff go long over time and are virtually impossible to understand. Is it laziness or stupidity that stops them preparing? The argument that this is only supposed to be a two-minute speech, so why prepare, falls over when the rambling speech becomes ten or fifteen minutes instead. The audience shuffle their feet, move in their seats and look as if they're in pain. When it's over they are happy and relieved, but ask each other: 'What did they say?'.

If a client of mine is to speak at a conference, I will be finding out from the conference organisers as much demographic information as possible about the conference attendees: age groups; income levels; position in the corporation; major qualifications; recent issues; expectations; and interests. I also want to know who the other speakers are and what their subject is. That way, my client can be delivering their message in a relevant way and in the audience's language. I will also try to be at the venue early, checking that seating, podium and sound system are all in place. When my client stands up to deliver a speech, it is too late to find out that there is no podium for speech notes or no microphone. A speech is a performance, and the best performances are well rehearsed.

WHAT MAKES A GOOD SPEECH?

There is some debate among the experts on what makes a good speech. Some claim that it's not what you say, it's how you say it. This school of thought says most of your effort should be put into preparation: knowing or memorising your information and practising. They emphasise that you should begin with confidence and finish with energy, in between varying your pitch, your pace and your expressions. For example, pauses are powerful. And, of course, this school of thought urges you to make eye contact and big, open hand gestures that reach towards your audience, instead of crossing your arms and closing yourself to them. This is all good advice, but it's only one side of the story.

> ... begin with confidence and finish with energy ...

Others focus on the reverse: it's not how you say it, it's what you say. Here content is the key, and stress is placed on repetition and reinforcement. Most speakers think repetition will bore audiences, but these experts claim audiences appreciate repetition because it helps them remember what you said. As part of repetition, your speech should frequently summarise what you have just said.

A third school of experts believe neither of the above points. Instead, they point to how you put your message together: the structure. A typical example here would be as follows. First, hook your listeners by beginning with what's on their mind. Second, focus on an issue they are dealing with that relates to their needs. Then you can present your recommendations, which are the key points you wanted to make in the first place. This should be a clear and simple statement. You can then elaborate on the benefits of your recommendation, whether it is an idea, a product or a service. Forget the features, because if your speech sells well the audience will come around for those later. These 'structural' experts also say you should then provide some evidence for your point of view, such as statistics, historical analogies, expert testimonies or case studies. Finally, they say, good speeches summarise the whole message and then finish with an appeal to the audience to take action.

All the experts agree that it is critically important to start your speech well. For business, community and conference speeches, I recommend you choose one of three ways to make a high-impact beginning:

- Tell a personal anecdote about how you link with the topic.
- Ask a question that is on the mind of the audience.
- Create a story and image from a classic movie or hit TV show.

The personal anecdote can be funny, but it's not necessary to make people laugh. In fact, joke telling is overrated and dangerous territory. Instead, your anecdotes can be straightforward. They could refer to a family holiday or an incident at work, and then lead into the topic. The point is not to go into too much detail, but start on a warm, friendly, personal note.

Asking a question is my favourite speech starter. This has been used and abused in politics, with the most famous being by presidential candidate Ronald Reagan, asking his audiences again and again when campaigning against President Carter: 'Are you better off today than you were four years ago?' In a community speech your could start with 'Are the streets and parks as attractive as they were for my grandparents?' or you could appeal to the hip-pocket nerve with 'Is your money working as hard as it should?'.

Telling a story from a classic movie or well-known TV show can reach most of your audience because these have a big general impact. You are simply borrowing their power and appeal. In a speech on the importance of honesty, call up a story from Seinfeld on the trouble George created when he chose to cover something up, rather than face the awkward truth. Instantly, the audience is on your wavelength.

A positive person will deliver messages with a sharp focus, honesty and simplicity, repetition and consistency, ultimately hitting the mark and winning the audience. The negative speaker's communication alienates the audience, allows no responses, leads nowhere and is a generally one-sided exercise. We've all heard lots like this. On the other hand, the positive person satisfies the audience, making them responsive. This speaker helps the audience move forward and the whole speech feels like a shared experience.

Let's go, then, to that moment when you stand at the front of the room and are about to deliver a speech. This is the moment that most people fear more than death, or so they say. What can get you through these vital seconds?

- Take a deep breath. It won't be deep enough, but try as hard as you can to take the deepest breath possible. Once you've done that, do it again. This will calm you, and make you look calm.
- Pause and look the audience in the eye. Most people think you must start talking straight away. This is not so. Instead, make eye contact.
- Look at the friendliest faces. Pick a few members of the audience to look at, and keep going to them. It is best to choose one from the middle of the room plus one up close. They don't know you are looking just at them. In fact, everyone in that section thinks your gaze is on them.

> ... the positive person satisfies the audience, making them responsive.

TIPS FOR VOICE AND BODY LANGUAGE

The UK Public Relations Consultants Association produced a useful *Guidance Paper on Presentation Skills*. Although it was published way back in 1986, it is so good I still give it to clients who have a speech to make. The guide provides the following tips for voice and body language in presentations.

Voice

Speed
When someone is nervous, they tend to speak too fast, drop the volume and speak in a flat tone. This is likely to make the audience think that what they have to say is boring.

Volume

What you need is a variety of volume. An increase in volume will emphasise points, and a decrease will invite the audience to listen carefully. You should speak louder than when carrying on a conversation. In the process, you will sound authoritative and enthusiastic.

Body language

Hands

Use your hands for emphasis and make the gestures bold. Do not put your hands in your pockets or on your hips and don't fold your arms. Do not fidget with pens, glasses or anything else.

Mannerisms

Mannerisms are things you may not be aware of, but should be avoided. They include rocking on your feet and running your hands through your hair. These only distract the audience from what you are saying.

Eye contact

Make each person in the room feel they are being personally addressed by making eye contact. Start each point by looking at one person, then scan the room as you continue. If you look out the window, gaze at the floor or scan the wall, you risk upsetting the audience.

Handling questions is a special art form. It is vitally important because when an audience asks questions it is a sign of interest: you have grabbed them and fired their imagination. Questions need to be welcomed and controlled during a presentation. The best approach is to thank the questioner; rephrase the question in your language; answer; check with the questioner that they are satisfied; and thank them for the question.

A final tip, which I have used with many clients, is to remember that you are more interesting than you think and you do know your subject, so tell it the best way you can. The audience really wants you to do well. Most audiences, hearing a well-prepared speech, are thankful that you have given them good communication. Plenty of other speakers will have bored them stupid.

IS THE CUSTOMER ALWAYS RIGHT? 23

'The customer is always right.' What a ridiculous statement! Do you know anybody who has always been right? Yet many business people hold to 'The customer is always right' as if it alone contains the secret of success. Like many clichés, this one contains a lot of truth, but it is only part of the story when it comes to success in sales, in building a corporate reputation or in advancing the cause of a community organisation.

These days, corporations have a broader definition of the customer. It could be the person on the other side of the store counter, but today 'customer' also includes work colleagues, members of the club, the community, parents of school children and more. All these are customers, though not in the sense that they are people making a purchase. For a community group, the people in a certain location may be the key to the group's success, so in that way they become customers. Many corporations are coming to realise that the word 'customer' can be applied broadly, rather than just to the point of sale. The question is: what is the best attitude to take to customers?

> ... the word 'customer' can be applied broadly, rather than just to the point of sale.

EFFECTIVE SALES COMMUNICATION

In evaluating the sales and communication effectiveness of salespeople, based on corporate experience I ask five questions.

1. **What is the general attitude of the salespeople I am dealing with?** If they appear to like people, that's a good start. If they are totally committed to success on our project, aim to do it right the first time and are actually interested in me, I am definitely ready to buy. People who are interested in others are generally happy within themselves, while failures in sales are often those who are pretty miserable anyway, with the lost sale further proof of their personal failure. Failure becomes a vicious circle, while success can be the circle of confidence, with happiness at the centre.

2. **Do I get a feeling of partnership with these salespeople?** Here I am looking for their commitment to telling the truth and actually consulting my needs. For example, have they asked me any questions?
3. **Will they solve problems?** Nobody likes to think a problem will arise. But, in anticipation that one may arise, it is good to deal with people who seem able to solve problems, and who treat them as challenging opportunities.
4. **Are the salespeople where I need them?** I want to buy from people who are available. Has their organisation reached out to me?
5. **Does the organisation apply people power to their salespeople?** If the people I deal with cannot make a decision, why go further?

Good selling is like good communication, and the starting point for both is asking questions so that you know what the other person wants, particularly when that other person influences your career. Good salespeople know that often the customer does not really know what they want. By asking questions, the salesperson can then guide the customer to the right solution. Knowing what the other person wants is the only way to have a hope of success.

> *... often the customer does not really know what they want.*

The way you deal with people becomes a huge factor in how they view you. In marketing terms, it helps you build value in your brand. You would expect a communicator to say this, but the importance of people in any organisation or transaction has been independently checked out in a major Gallup Organisation study. Gallup's Dr Bill McEwen reported in June 2000 that there is consistent and powerful evidence that it is people who play a key role in building customer brand loyalty. The study looked at the importance of differentiators (such as location, price and advertising), which are often thought to be the key ways to create a brand difference. It looked at these in three sectors where there is said to be a sameness about the product or service: domestic airline travel; long-distance telephone service; and cheque accounts at banks. Interestingly, many of the brands in these industries have used differentiators such as price, location and advertising to make them stand out from the competition and build their brand. Gallup went to customers and evaluated differentiators such as product, price, place and promotions, and they added to this list the importance of people. Has brand-building worked when based on differentiators like price and advertising?

> *... it is people who play a key role in building customer brand loyalty.*

In the airline category, Gallup found that price and product were not significant loyalty drivers for customers. Factors such as accessibility and schedule convenience were important, as would be expected. But the really dramatic finding is described by Dr McEwen:

> *More important than schedule convenience—and as much as three or four times more important than brand advertising—are the people on the ground and in the air who 'touch' the customer. Customers who report that an airline's employees stand out are up to fifteen times more likely to say they will choose that airline the next time they fly.*

In airlines the key is people. This is what can make or break the brand. Good people providing good service make customers come back for more. This highlights how important it is for airlines and other corporations to know how effectively they are communicating, and to ensure that their communication and people skills are right. Communication should even be listed as an asset or liability on their balance sheet, so investors know where they stand.

When it comes to long-distance telephone calls, the findings were somewhat different. The price or value is a major driver for customer loyalty, with those who believe they are being provided excellent value being two to four times more likely to say they would stay with that provider. When the study turned to people, it followed the airline trend: customers who feel the employees of their long-distance service provider are exceptional are eight to twelve times more likely to stay with that provider. As Dr McEwen put it: 'When we looked at what motivates customer retention, the company's employees are actually three to four times more important than the perceived value of the service'.

It turned out to be a similar story in banking. For some banks, location and convenience were factors and advertising reinforced the customer commitment. But the number one driver again is people, with customers who feel that a bank's employees stand out being far more likely—as much as ten to twenty times—to indicate that they would keep their cheque account at that bank.

Dr McEwen sums up: 'This is consistent—and powerful—evidence that people play a key role in building customer brand loyalty.'

CREATING REAL SALES COMMUNICATION

These findings highlight the stupidity of the age-old belief that the customer is always right. It is stupid because, first and foremost, the customer is a human being. People are not always right. In fact, many are more often wrong than right. That's human. Ask yourself: is anyone always right? Of course not. Being human, we will all make mistakes. Even customers make mistakes. So to be highly trained into believing that the customer is always right will make you a bit of a robotic slave. It may help you communicate with some people, but with others your stance will be seen as greasy and predetermined, as if you are being nice just to get a sale.

I suspect my view on the futility of believing the customer is always right would have been shared by one of the founders of the US advertising industry, Albert Lasker, who lived from 1880 to 1952. Like me, Lasker started out in journalism and spent much of his career developing techniques to use communication to change opinions. In advertising, he built one of the US's leading firms on the belief that advertising was salesmanship in print. Having started his life in words, it was perhaps predictable that Lasker held the view that all the agency had to do was write advertising copy that sold the product. He had little respect for art directors and design, areas that today play a dominant role in brand development. He did have the capacity to understand the customer and think outside the square.

> **Even customers make mistakes.**

Kotex (makers of women's sanitary napkins) sought Lasker's advice because their business was not growing as fast as they wanted. Rather than take the traditional advertising approach of carrying out research and development, Lasker and a few of his senior people went home and asked their wives if they used Kotex. They found that they didn't and in almost every case it was because they did not like to stand at the counter and ask out loud for the product. Yet that was the only way to buy Kotex. So Lasker didn't bother with issues of whether the customer was right or how the customer's behaviour could be changed. Instead, he used commonsense. He developed the simple idea of putting the Kotex in plain-wrapped packages on the counter so that women could walk in, grab the package, pay for it and walk out without any embarrassment. The business boomed, because commonsense prevailed.

I am calling for a revolution in thinking on sales communication. When sales meets customer, it is simply communication between two or more people. Now that most of us are in some form of sales role, we should think of ourselves less as reps and more as ambassadors for the company. Everything we say and do will have a positive or negative impact on the reputation of the company. We cannot afford to make a sale with slick techniques that, in the long term, damage the reputation of the business. Closing the deal and using opening lines should be thrown out of the manuals. They make the salesperson seem less than human, and make customers feel the same.

What is the alternative? What should our revolution in thinking on sales communication achieve? Now that most of us have sales as part of our role, how should we approach the task? Here are my ten steps towards a new type of sales communication:

- Be obviously honest and sincere.
- Tell the truth, always.
- Treat people with respect and as valuable human beings.
- Be interested in people, not just in your product. Learn a little philosophy as well as human psychology.
- Think more about your target audience.
- Obtain trust through relationships.
- Know and study your product and the competition, so you can speak about both as a genuine expert. People are after your expertise, not your sales patter.
- Forget all you learned at charm school or at the 'go get 'em' sales training program.
- Become a real listener, not just the kind who is thinking about their next line.
- Have a genuinely compassionate and caring attitude towards your customers.

Selling is basic to the success of an organisation, so if you are in sales you are a vital part of the organisation and your statements contribute positively or negatively to that organisation's overall reputation or image. Anyone who tells lies in order to gain a short-term sale sends the organisation and themselves on a downward spiral. On the other hand, in all business situations and in community groups, you can use some genuine sales techniques to gain the agreement of others, win support or overcome any opposition. Many of us in our community groups or workplaces find ourselves trying to sell ideas and concepts, often with little success. For some reason, we don't have the right patter to win people over. By using certain phrases, you can learn to improve your patter and win more people to your point of view. Some of these phrases are:

> *... your statements contribute positively or negatively to that organisation's overall reputation or image.*

- 'Something you said to me last week has prompted me to develop this concept . . . What do you think?'
- 'If we don't do this, I feel that some of our competitors will.'
- 'I've scanned the competition and am sure that nobody else could do this as well as we could.'
- 'Time is a real problem here. I would like more, but we haven't got long to consider this idea. It's basically now or never.'

Negotiating is a part of sales; it is also part of everyday life. For people in sales, negotiation becomes almost a way of life. All good negotiators have first-class communication skills. Negotiation is simply a high form of communication, so good negotiators are good communicators. They can put their case or product forward clearly and quickly understand where the other side is coming from. The best negotiators are well prepared prior to the negotiation, increasing their chances of success. They are attentive listeners and capable of establishing rapport. They know their own product or service, and have some knowledge of the person or organisation they are trying to convince.

The key stages in better selling and negotiating are much the same:

- Plan your strategy and approach.
- Make sure you know your side, and theirs.
- Put forward your proposal.
- Listen for the response and begin a debate.
- Bargain with the other side—give and take.
- Sum up—ratify the result.

> ... good negotiators are good communicators.

The best sales and negotiations are based around needs: the needs of the other person or the other organisation. Good salespeople are good listeners and have the ability to adapt their offer to what the other side is thinking. As you talk, different needs could emerge, so you need to be a good listener and an adaptable salesperson. Avoid overstating or understating your product or case, and instead value honesty and accuracy. If, for example, you exaggerate the benefits of a product or service, pretty soon the buyer will be disappointed and go somewhere else. Take the attitude that life goes on, and that this is one sale or one negotiation in a lifetime, so regard every action as building the long-term relationship.

> ... you need to be a good listener and an adaptable salesperson.

How can you replace the 'customer is always right' myth? How can you achieve the kind of breakthrough that came naturally to Albert Lasker? Sales is fundamentally about communication, and communication holds the secrets for better customer relations. It starts with your mind. Deal with the customer in a negative way (lack confidence, be closed, be afraid, and have a chattering mind with thoughts everywhere) and you will make them feel edgy too, so the sale falls through. You have a better chance of success if your mind is controlled, you are self-assured, open and friendly, and see the customer as they really are.

With your mind in the positive, you can create messages that get across. With a negative start, your messages become confusing, you use riddles or even deceit, your line varies and you are uncertain.

But with a positive mind you can ensure your messages have sharp focus and clarity, are honest and simple, are repeated and consistent, and hit the mark. You and the customer will be making eye contact, nodding in agreement and getting on like friends instead of standing off like adversaries.

There will be lots of feedback, some positive and some negative. Any feedback is good feedback, because it builds the foundation for your next communication. That is why you should welcome negative feedback just as much as the positive. If you treat the customer in a robotic way or with a closed mind or send confusing messages, then feedback is likely to be unsatisfying. There may even be a nil response, or when it occurs it leads nowhere. The whole exchange will seem one-sided. But you can expect more creative sales feedback when your mind and messages hit the mark. The communication will get a response, you and they will seem satisfied, you will both see the way forward and the whole process will have been a shared experience. This is what customers are looking for: sales, yes, but with real communication.

The question is: can you do it? Can you move beyond simplistic thinking, such as 'The customer is always right', and create a real communication with all your customers, basing sales on open and shared communication? If you do not have the skills of communication, you will be unlikely to succeed. If you are unhappy, you have little chance of success in any field, but most certainly not in sales. If you feel desperate for a change and believe people don't understand you, if your main focus is yourself and you always have a nagging feeling of missing out, you will be a poor communicator and a poor salesperson. Unhappiness creates barriers between people. It stifles communication, creating isolation. Sales thrive in a climate of friendship, fun and openness. You can make the change if you are happy: feeling that you have what you want, that people generally understand you, that you like to think of others and that you have a general sense of contentment. None of this rules out having personal drive and ambition.

> *. . . you should welcome negative feedback just as much as the positive.*

> *Sales thrive in a climate of friendship, fun and openness.*

The good news here is that so much of success in sales and in building a brand comes down to people. As an individual, you don't need to be wealthy, successful or wear the right clothes to create sales and success; you just need to be you. The better your communication, the more accurate your brand will be because people will understand you. For corporations and community groups, the Gallup findings are also good news because they are a reminder that people are your biggest asset, and that working on internal and external communication has a real purpose. Not to communicate is to leave things to chance; taking steps to improve communication can actually reduce the risks you face. It will give you greater impact in sales and more success in whatever you do for customers.

THINK OF THE FUTURE AS E-LIFE

24

Business executives are now spending about the same time on email as they do on meetings, representing one of the most radical changes in work practice in decades. To do well in an Internet environment, you will need to improve your communication skills. Does this sound like a contradiction? The information revolution is only a revolution in how we deliver information; you still need to be a good communicator. In fact, some believe the information revolution means you have to be even better at getting your message across. For example, look at how this new technology brings your writing skills to the fore. People who used to dictate letters and hide behind secretaries are now exposed as virtually illiterate through their emails.

> *... the average respondent spends 123 minutes per day using email ...*

Communication consultancies Rogen International and Goldhaber Research Associates surveyed 1400 executives. They found that the average respondent spends 123 minutes per day using email and 136 minutes in face-to-face meetings. Not bad, considering five years ago they might have spent zero time on emails. That is, executives rate meetings as one of their major tasks, but they spend just thirteen minutes less on emails than they do on face-to-face meetings. According to Rogen, knowing when to communicate electronically and when to actually talk to someone is fast becoming a new test of leadership potential. The email is one of the big tests you face as you seek to advance your career. For example, Rogen advises that, while it is a lot easier to send bad news via email, from a long-term, leadership perspective it is not an option. It is far better to convey bad news face to face. On the other hand, according to Rogen, email 'turbo boosts communication as a whole'. They estimate that usage is up 77 per cent on 2000, and that four trillion emails will be sent in 2001 from 600 million electronic mailboxes.

Ford use the Internet to tell staff where they want the business to go and how it is going. They claim to have the world's largest intranet. Their purpose-built newsroom maintains the website, which is updated several times a day. Ford understand the importance of talking to staff and how the Internet can help them talk better. In keeping with this, they give employees computers to use at home so they will adopt online thinking, while being accessible for consistent global messages. Ford have also added a scheme to allow the friends or family of an employee to buy a company vehicle at a discount via the Internet, faster and easier than rival company schemes.

SAP, a German software giant, is another company using this new communication. They have a system allowing material to be broadcast on the car radios of workers on the road. All this talk with employees is called 'B2E' (business to employee) and this is a growth area of corporate communications. Basic communication is extended to include many human resources services, creation of internal job markets and use of the Internet for training.

New technology has greatly increased the choices for communication, with our desks becoming superb message centres. Information can be received and relayed, from our desk, anywhere around the world. The key remains to take a human approach. While e-commerce has been seen as cold, standing for the application of technology to business, the future must embrace the concept of 'e-life': the application of technology and innovation to our lives, public and private. Here is the human factor. The revolution may be technology-based but, at the end of the day, it is about people, and how we get on with each other. Communication is an important part of new technology.

> *The key remains to take a human approach.*

IMPROVING THE POWER OF YOUR EMAILS

Emails are fast, user-friendly (easy) and versatile. Email has become a prime medium of communication within our businesses and is quickly taking over from the letter in our personal lives. One of the best tips I have heard is to use a meaningful and persuasive subject title, because this is what the reader at the other end sees when they are deciding whether or not to read your email. Put some sell into the subject title and they are more likely to open your message.

Think about how to communicate using this new technology to build relationships and positively affect your career. For example, you will communicate better through email if you:

- Use bullet point summaries.
- Keep it short.
- Attach anything that is detailed, so the reader can choose whether or not to read it.

- Include questions—this ensures you get a response.
- Be relaxed and friendly in style.

A good rule for all communication applies even more so to email: never use obscene language or insults and shun any racist or sexist mail.

The use of a question is terrific in any verbal or written communication. It guides your subject to what is expected of them and turns your one message into the beginning of a dialogue. If you include a question you are less likely to be ignored.

Promotion will not be just around the corner if your emails to the boss contain lots of spelling errors, appear chaotic and leave them wondering what the communication was all about. On the other hand, a short, snappy and effective message can work well for you.

With all this technology, do not overlook the art of persuasion. Are you communicating to get something, change something or create something? If you are, whether communicating face to face or via email, you will need to be persuasive. For example, in using email it is very important to make your messages 'human'. They need to reflect your personality and express how you feel. An email message that reads like a bureaucratic report will fail to get the right response. But add some passion and commitment to show that you believe in what you are saying, and people are ready to receive your message.

> *... in using email it is very important to make your messages 'human'.*

Persuasion also occurs best when two people find common ground. That is, your email messages must be framed so they appeal to the target audience. This may involve getting some early feedback from them so you know what they think and how they feel about the topic. Then you can craft your next email message in language that appeals to them. The best communicators are good listeners. They focus on the concerns of others, tailoring their message to those concerns.

Boring people and boring messages are never persuasive. You do not get your message across by boring people. This applies as much to email as to other forms of communication. Don't be afraid to use vivid language or to express something strongly. Facts are important, but they need to be spiced up with some emotion.

> *... develop your communication step by step, allowing for feedback and change as you go.*

Avoid the hard sell in your first email on a topic. If you take a strong position straight away, it gives potential opponents something to oppose, and plenty of time to oppose it. Instead, develop your communication step by step, allowing for feedback and change as you go. Because email is such a responsive medium, it is ideal for this step-by-step delivery of a message or a point of view. Taking things one step at a time means you carry people along with you, rather than hit them with the lot and risk leaving them behind. Another great part of human communication is give and take. Again, the speed of email allows for plenty of this, so long as you craft your messages to be simple and open and to invite comment. We admire people who are prepared to compromise and to take notice of our concerns. In this way, you gain a shared understanding, which is one of the best ways to get a message across. Persuasion may take time, so don't just send one email message and think the job is done. It may take others a little longer than hoped to come around to your view. It is better to communicate, listen, test your view, and then listen, compromise and communicate again, then listen, and so on. Persuasion is generally a process involving many steps of communication.

Three good tips for using email more effectively are:

- Send only essential messages, particularly in business.
- Keep messages short.
- Avoid delays in replying.

It is a good idea to get into the habit of using the email 'reply' function to force yourself to respond immediately. Those wanting to succeed in business need to realise that email and the Internet have placed them in a fishbowl. Eric Schmidt, Chief Executive of Novell, says that if you have failed to reply to an email you can no longer hide behind 'My secretary lost the message'. Schmidt continues: 'I have to assume that every bit of information about me is broadcast back to our employees and customers'.

IMPROVING YOUR E-COMMUNICATION

Dave, my tennis mate, has a Masters in Computer Science and is building some of the best websites in the country. He has never studied marketing and he does not read much. His approach to work is the same as his approach to the tennis court (his major recreation): he plays fast and hard and lets his racquet do the talking. He rarely speaks at client meetings and does virtually no writing. Some say he is a poor communicator, and to many he is seen as the quiet person in the office. But Dave's websites work like marketing machines. How does he do it?

Dave is successful in IT because he picks the brains of the best in marketing and communication. While doing his Masters, he was playing tennis with a marketing expert and they chatted about the future, email, the Web and Internet business. This was Dave's chosen direction, so he listened intently to his tennis buddy. Dave tells it this way:

We were sitting by the edge of the court, sweaty and tired, having a short break before starting another doubles match. My friend was talking about market segments and lots of technical stuff. Then he said something that I have used mercilessly with every client on every site. He said the key question to consider before creating any Web business is: why would anyone bother to visit this site? To me, he had cut through the complexity and provided the best piece of advice for me, and ultimately for everyone I have created a site for. We never start to build any aspect of a site until we know the answer to that question.

In fact, as Dave develops sites for clients and the relationship grows, he is the one who keeps drawing the team back to that question: why would anybody bother to visit? In so doing, he has displayed an innate knowledge of communication, where sharp focus and clarity make for good communication. He has shown awareness that communication works if it satisfies oneself and others, while too many who create websites are thinking only of their own egos. He is allowing people to be responsive. These considerations are important in your personal communication. Asking why people would communicate with you is a good, although sometimes scary, beginning point for better communication.

> **... communication works if it satisfies oneself and others ...**

All successful marketing, communication and sales creates a conversation with the customer, whether this conversation is in person, by staff, over the phone, through direct mail or via the Web. Creators of this 'conversation' theory point back to the earliest marketplaces in history, where people came to their village market to buy, trade and meet each other. All three—buy, trade and meet—were important in the success of these markets. As we moved to mass marketing and mass communication, we forgot this system. But with the arrival of the Web, marketers and consumers alike now see the re-creation of the old village market where conversation took place. Now on the Web, customers can check price, monitor performance and share information with people like ourselves. Lots of talk is happening and lots of comparisons are being made. In this funny way, perhaps the Web is reminding us all of the basics of communication and the importance of conversation.

> **You need to remember that conversations only occur if someone is listening ...**

You need to remember that conversations only occur if someone is listening, and too many companies are good at talking and poor at listening. Eventually customers ignore them, and the scary thing about the Web is that people can choose to ignore you sooner.

Tips from the website makers

Some of the considerations that Dave and his IT colleagues apply to the Web can help you improve your communication.

Ask why customers would bother to come to this site
If the experience of visiting your website is not valuable to the customer, they will not come back. It is the same in personal life; if you are not responsive and giving, eventually people will stop making an effort to communicate with you.

For website makers, it is important to ask questions constantly, including what do we want customers to do when they visit our site and why would they come back? One of Dave's more obvious questions is to clients who take a 'me too' approach to their website and tell him they want a site just like their competitor. He asks: 'If your site is just like the competition, why would people choose to come to you?'. The message behind all this is that the value in a site is not in the pictures and technomagic—though these can be important. The value is in what the customer can do and what you deliver.

At a personal level, this means you should not be afraid to be different, to avoid following the pack. In fact, it is the things that make you different that make you interesting to others.

Ask why customers would choose this site over a competitor's
In business, marketing communication is what sets you apart. The purpose is to create a point of difference, especially a point of difference you know customers want. These values need to be reflected in websites.

> . . . think through all the possible reasons a person may visit your site.

It is also important to think through all the possible reasons a person may visit your site. With the Web, you can't see them coming through the door, or locate yourself in the young, trendy end of town. In other words, the normal demographics do not apply so much, especially at point of entry. So you need a Web system to establish quickly why people have come to the site.

At a personal level, the message here is to be responsive and think about the other person. By doing so, you become better at getting your message across.

> . . . the key is to make it easy to find and choose what customers want.

Make it easy, then make it easier
Customers are not researchers. Most will not have the skills to navigate their way around a complex site. A successful website provides the right level of information and, for some

services, that means providing an information-rich format. Even there the key is to make it easy to find and choose what customers want. One of the dangers of having too much graphic design input into a site is that every page and every section can finish up having a different 'look'. This may be pleasing to the designer's eye but it is confusing for visitors. Consistency above creativity is a good starting point.

What works for the Web can work for you. Make it easy for people to talk with you and you will find that they will; put up obstacles or complexity and they will go away.

Relate it to the rest of your business
For most companies and organisations, a website becomes an additional channel for information and products. It does not replace existing channels, so it makes sense for the site to complement the other ways you do business. For example, ask: How does it fit in with our sales and business development team? Should it relate to storefront outlets? An aspect of relating your site to the rest of your business is its 'look'. The best websites look the same as the other visual representations of the company. Visitors who have gone to the site because they have a relationship with you and trust you do not want to be surprised by a completely foreign look for the site. It should look like the rest of you: logos, brochures, in-store merchandise and so on.

> **The best websites look the same as the other visual representations of the company.**

This website lesson works well for the individual because it highlights the need to be consistent and true to yourself. If your communication is varied and jumps all over the place (probably in a failed effort to impress somebody) then ultimately it breaks down. If you follow the Web approach, you present a consistent message to the outside world and people come to understand you at a deeper level.

In 1998 four marketing and corporate management 'mavericks'—Rick Levine, Christopher Locke, Doc Searls and David Weinberger—used a website to launch 'The Cluetrain Manifesto', which ridiculed the conventional wisdom about marketing and management. For example, they said, 'Most marketing programs are based on a fear that the market might see what's really going on inside the company'. Isn't this so true of many people you know? Maybe it is partly true about you. The authors show how this fear ultimately stifles success and communication, so you had better believe too that if you are hiding your real self from others, you are heading for communication failure. The four later produced a book, *The Cluetrain Manifesto: The End of Business as Usual* (Perseus Books, 2000).

173

The Web is a key part of the future of communications for many purposes, whether at a business, community or personal level. It's even replacing the postcard, particularly when people visit isolated places. Friends of mine recently spent time in an isolated part of South America, but kept in touch through regular emails sent from small townships. Even in isolated areas the Web can bring us together. But saying it once via email is not enough; communication really only happens when your email elicits a reply or some positive action. So you should see your email not as a job well done, but just the beginning of better communication.

PART 5

Creativity and spirit: communicating for a better tomorrow

25 Communication and the human spirit   177
26 Some old-fashioned advice   185
27 You can be a creative communicator   190

COMMUNICATION AND THE HUMAN SPIRIT 25

Are we asking the 'Who am I' question more these days? There seems to be a growing interest in the link between everything we do (work, sport, leisure) and the human spirit. Corporate executives are asking the question, and so even some companies are reviewing how they treat people, who they are and where they are going. Much is being written on this topic and the workplace, with some business spokespersons using phrases such as 'spiritual renaissance'. Others are saying 'Let's get back to talking', while some highlight the importance of 'making a life, not just a living'. The head of Saatchi & Saatchi is talking about 'lovemarks' instead of 'brands' and his firm regards business transactions as 'conversations'. This is soft language in the hard world of business. Modern corporations, closely watching the growing interest in the human spirit, are keen to know what modern people want and are intrigued by what brings happiness.

The *Oxford Dictionary* defines 'spirit' as the 'animating or vital principle of man; the intelligent or immaterial part of man'. It describes 'spiritual' as 'of the soul'. It's worth looking at how it defines 'communicate'. It is to 'impart, transmit, have social dealings with, succeed in conveying information'. Both words ('spirit' and 'communicate') refer to something largely invisible, something we can't hold or touch. Despite this, they are always there. From these definitions alone, we can see the potential links between the human spirit and communication.

As wars and other tough times have shown, during periods of change and stress the human spirit and communication become even more important, as we cling to core values against the external turbulence. My grandfather used to talk about the way families helped each other during the hard years of the Great Depression. If one family grew too many potatoes, they passed the excess on to someone without. Wallets were empty, but for many the human spirit was full. Even so, the toll of the Depression was so great that it destroyed the spirit and lives of many people.

Given that most of us know that money isn't everything, that the human spirit is far more important, that communication is better than power, why, then, do we forget these beliefs in so many aspects of our lives? When we go to work, we seem to leave these values at the door. When our social relationships are tested, we forget the strength of these values. At home, we often put our humanity aside. Is it because we think spirit and communication are too soft for these 'tough', real-life situations?

Perhaps money does buy happiness? Most Americans tell the Gallup Organisation that they would like to be rich. Over 75 per cent of students entering college in the USA now consider it 'very important' or even 'essential' that they become 'very well off financially'. This is three out of four: double the number in 1970. Our interest and belief in money seems to be going up. But is the belief matched by the research? Does being rich make us happier? University of Michigan researcher Ronald Inglehart found from a sixteen-nation study of 170 000 people that the correlation between income and happiness is 'surprisingly weak'. He found that once people are comfortable (have food, clothing and shelter) more money provides diminishing returns. The second chocolate, the second million dollars, never satisfies as much as the first. It seems that the absence of wealth can create misery, but having it does not guarantee happiness.

Against this background, Saatchi & Saatchi have been re-evaluating the meaning of 'brand' and the power of communication. They are highly critical of much of business communication for its lack of real humanity. As Sandra Yates, Chairperson of Saatchi & Saatchi Australia, says, corporations need to reinvent conversations: 'Reinventing conversations means that we accept the importance of a two-way dialogue and that we start to listen with understanding'. It all sounds very human, rather than commercial. But Yates believes it is essential to commercial success:

> ... the correlation between income and happiness is 'surprisingly weak'.

> Most business communication these days focuses on telling people things we want them to know. A conversation, by contrast, is an opportunity to find out what people would like to know about us, and then to tailor a response that has the potential to drive us a significant strategic edge.

She warns her business audience that 'People don't trust anyone who doesn't listen to them, who they don't understand, or who they think is taking advantage of them'.

RECOGNISING OTHERS AS HUMAN BEINGS

If the conversation revolution has begun in business, it is purely because of a belated recognition that we are not consumers, we are human beings. The human spirit is being noticed in boardrooms. Yates concludes:

We must stop telling, and start asking. We must stop answering questions nobody asked, and try to figure out the real questions people want us to respond to. We need to develop our listening skills, and every communication should be in the language of our customers, not the language of business.

There's a lesson in this corporate message. We can all play a part in the conversation revolution and find that our human spirit will soar as a result. That work colleague is not just a specialist we can talk to only when we need them, but also a person. That member of the tennis club is not just a player, but also a person like us with hopes, families, loneliness and views. If all we value is their tennis game, we have missed the human spirit: theirs and ours. That person serving us at the local market is not just a shop assistant, but also a person and one who is helping us. We owe them the right to be human. We will all communicate better if we recognise that our friends and colleagues are people, and that like us they have a spirit and desire for communication. Treating everybody we contact as a valuable human being is not a novel concept, but it is not often spoken of today. This thinking can lift us out of the ordinary. We will accept that how a person plays, works or relates cannot be separated from their sense of self. The more we know about this other person's self, the better will be our communication.

How can we communicate in this conversation revolution? Taking some of the pointers from the new business communication, your communication will be vastly better if you:

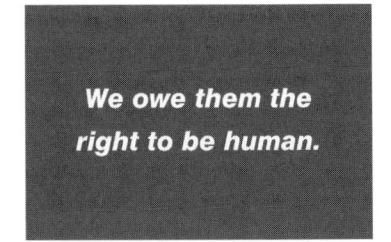

> **We owe them the right to be human.**

- Accept that everybody has something to contribute.
- Encourage others to join in, rather than stay apart.
- Build and earn trust.
- Flow with the changes of life, while pushing towards improvement.
- Always look at people with eyes wide open, ready for the unexpected, rather than taking them for granted.
- Be ready to give feedback, preferably more good than bad.

DANGERS OF THE 'BLAMING COMMUNITY'

One of the most powerful ideas in the western world today is, if something goes wrong, someone else must be to blame. We have become the 'blame community', instead of the real community. Simon Longstaff, Executive Director of St James Ethics Centre in Sydney, suggests that blaming others often misses the point. He is critical of the modern attitude where, 'Its focus is the autonomous individual and its signature is the assignment of blame—not necessarily where the fault lies, but where the capacity for compensation is greatest'. As he points out, with good fortune most of us will pass our lives without tragedy. But, for some, life is blighted by events that defy understanding and explanation. Longstaff explains:

> It might be the unexpected death of a child, or the loss of all one's possessions in a flood, or an injury sustained simply from being in the wrong place at the wrong time. In these circumstances we are naturally inclined to look for someone or something to blame.

As Longstaff points out, in the past there used to be many scapegoats, including a 'pantheon of malign spirits' or just plain bad luck. The key here, Longstaff says, is that, 'Whatever the specific pattern of blame, it often reflected a common sense that some things were beyond the control of individuals'. Just as corporations seem to be moving to greater humanisation of their communication, we as individuals seem to be moving away, looking for people or corporations to blame. Longstaff suggests that:

> Perhaps the urge to blame the individual and extract our pound of flesh can be linked to a palpable loss of our sense of community. If the person who suffers is not our neighbour, then why not leave them to bleed on the side of the road? If we do not feel like a community, then how can we be motivated to share the cost of helping those whom life has wounded?

Longstaff uses an example to show how far the 'someone is to blame' phenomenon can go: if an arsonist uses a candle to burn down a house, perhaps the hapless candlestick maker is liable to be sued. Reflecting an understanding of the human spirit, he concludes with this call:

> The unhappy truth is that when bad things happen it is not always because someone is at fault. One option may be to vent our fury at whatever or whoever comes to mind. Another might be to recognise our interdependence and give life to our sense of community. Rub-a-dub-dub; we're all in this tub.

HUMANISATION OF COMMUNICATION

These days the hard-nosed brand experts are reflecting Longstaff's view that we are all in this together. They are starting to use mushy language, and even use the previously forbidden four-letter word: love. They identify the previously unspoken attribute of happiness as a key factor in successful communication; they see love as part of brand loyalty. Kevin Roberts, global CEO of Saatchi & Saatchi, makes a distinction between values and spirit. He urges brands to move towards love, which he says is truly important for making connections with consumers. He says that love is: 'Where the human spirit resides in the

> ... they see love as part of brand loyalty.

worlds of our own dreams and aspirations. Ideas, great ideas, do their work in the heart and in the gut. Once you have that, their minds will follow'. If corporations are moving towards things like love and spirit, then we as human beings should be able to reclaim this ground too.

Only a minority of corporations heeds the messages on communication, humanity and brand. Many either disappoint or mistreat customers, failing to worry about the cost of poor service. Dissatisfied customers, we know, mostly just go somewhere else, not even bothering to let the business know that they are unhappy. Some companies are changing what they call the 'brand experience'. Michael Silverstein, a senior vice-president in The Boston Consulting Group, has worked on developing the flawless brand experience. He says:

> *A handful of innovative companies are pioneering a different way of going to market. They are focusing on customers' experience with their brand and on building a reputation for pleasing them with flawless products or services. They are training their sales associates to understand that nothing less than impeccable performance is acceptable, and that bonuses, promotions, and shared profits will be based on rigorously quantified results.*

Silverstein is critical of many of today's research tools that fail to capture the nuances of how customers feel and to get to the heart of how customers experience a brand. Again, these are strange words from corporate marketing: feelings and the heart. It is certainly important for companies to keep customers. The Boston Consulting Group has found that it costs four to ten times the margin of their first purchase to acquire a new customer. The group tells their clients to create a flawless brand experience by tearing down the barriers between their organisation and the customer. To do this, the group believes companies must:

- Map customers' purchases and purchasing cycles.
- Identify areas for improvement.
- Design a better process, including specific steps to make contacts flawless.
- Measure performance customer by customer.
- Instil a vision of perfection in all associates; reward excellence.

They've set a tough standard for communication, brand and customer service. But when it could take four to ten purchases from one new customer to equal the cost of attracting them, it pays to keep customers.

Behind much of what The Boston Consulting Group is telling its clients is a message about customers being human beings, and the importance of treating them as such. They say that much of the money and energy spent on traditional views of brand (that it is about positioning, advertising, packaging, catchy logos and slogans) is wasted. Their view is that brand is about the 'total experience' a customer has with your products or services. They see this total experience in terms of 'enticing customers, gaining their trust, and making the experience so pleasant that they are proud of their choice and will tell others about it'. Their view is that because consumers are bombarded by advertising on TV and radio, in the newspapers, in bus shelters, on billboards and even on the Internet, they are tuning out. The group believes that when these advertising messages do get through, they are usually received with scepticism. This is tough news for traditional advertising agencies and their clients, looking to flog messages rather than considering the humanity of the consumer.

So much of this love and happiness message is coming from corporations when you would expect to hear it more from our spiritual leaders. Despite falling church attendance in much of the west, traditional churches such as Catholic and Anglican have done little to evaluate and change their form of communication. Gaining rising attendance are those churches that value communication; the evangelical movements such as the Baptists have experienced rising Sunday attendance. Some parts of the traditional church have turned things around by changing their behaviour. For example, a report for Springboard, the Archbishop of Canterbury's initiative to spread evangelical techniques in the UK, found that the best path to growth was through an outreach program such as the Alpha course, an introductory course on Christianity. Over 550 churches run the Alpha course and over a million people in Britain have done the course; a quarter of these have become active Christians. Perhaps this success will encourage other churches to adopt better communication techniques, and think more of their congregation as people, rather than thinking first of their own institution. As for corporations, being inward looking is a recipe for failure; going out and speaking to people as real human beings is the beginning of success.

> ... brand is about the 'total experience' a customer has with your products or services.

Out of change can come great benefit; the fact that the leader of the Tibetan people, His Holiness the Dalai Lama, had to go into exile in Northern India has led to a flowering of interest in Tibetan Buddhism. His messages stress the human spirit, with a special focus on how we are all interdependent:

> In our world, we need a clear awareness of the interdependent nature of nations, of humans and animals, and of humans, animals and the world. Everything is of interdependent nature. I feel that many problems, especially man-made problems, are due to a lack of knowledge about this interdependent nature.

His Holiness reminds us of the importance of defining happiness as we strive for it. He says: 'Happiness is a state of mind. With physical comforts if your mind is still in a state of confusion and agitation, it is not happiness. Happiness means calmness of mind'.

Even the management consultants are starting to use phrases such as 'love the job' and are advising companies that keeping good employees means keeping them satisfied, which involves more than a good salary. PricewaterhouseCoopers has studied this area and found that 20–30 per cent of elite skilled workers change jobs every year, while one in three people regret their first career choice. (This survey found that accountants were the most disgruntled.) A survey of 7500 workers in the USA by Watson Wyatt found that companies with highly committed employees had a 112 per cent three-year total return to shareholders, compared with a 76 per cent return for companies with low employee commitment. The message to company directors is that there are real dollars to be made out of communicating well, treating people as people and increasing your corporate concern for the human spirit.

US researcher, author and consultant Tom Terez has researched the search for fulfilment in the workplace. In 1997, he created Meaning At Work, a project that came up with a list of key factors creating meaningful work experiences. As you read these, think of how many involve human values and communication. On top of the list is purpose. Other factors are ownership, fit, oneness, relationship building, service quality, validation, invention, and personal development. Others are acknowledgment, challenge, dialogue, direction, flexibility, informality, relevance, respect, self-identity and support.

> . . . there are real dollars to be made out of communicating well . . .

LESSONS FROM THE NEW CORPORATE SPIRIT

What lessons can the individual draw from these companies, religions and consultants? How can you gain the best combination of happiness and communication? I have extracted eight key points from this surge in corporate talk of 'loving brands' and the human spirit:

- Accept change in your life and adapt to it. Don't postpone happiness until you have 'made it'. Strive to make wealth, but be happy as you go.
- Take progress in little bits, moment by moment, rather than looking for the great personal leap forward.
- Increase your feelings of being in control of your life by thinking about how you spend your time, and relating it to what you want.
- Put on a happy face. It seems that acting happy creates a happy frame of mind. Smile, you feel good; frown, you feel bad. It's not too

intellectual or clever, but remember that you are just a human being.
- Stick to the flow. If work is right and leisure is right, your spirit has time to soar. Researchers are using the word 'flow' to describe the zone where happy people are absorbed in their tasks and their life. They have found that expensive leisure, such as sailing a huge yacht, can produce less flow than gardening.
- Make connections and get on the move. Meeting people and getting some exercise are a fantastic combination for health and happiness. If you need more convincing of these, you just don't want to be happy.
- Give priority to those you love. Treat your closest people as special—remember them, make time for them, confide in them and share with them.
- Think of the human spirit. In so many studies, people who think about the spirit are happier and cope better. They also have a sense of self and community, some idea about the meaning of life and a better perspective.

A final word: if you do not like yourself, people will probably agree with your judgment.

SOME OLD-FASHIONED ADVICE

26

Speech is the most important of the communication tools available to us. But just because we know how to speak does not mean that we have the skills of speech. Good communication is not about turning all of us into a Nelson Mandela, Winston Churchill or Germaine Greer. Having the skills does not necessarily mean you become a great orator. It does mean that you know when and how to speak. Knowing when and how to speak is a basis for getting your message across. The good news is that we can all learn the skill of better speech, and much of this is based on some old-fashioned commonsense.

> *Knowing when and how to speak is a basis for getting your message across.*

THE RIGHT WORDS, AT THE RIGHT TIME

My grandmother used to put it this way: 'If you can't say something nice, say nothing'. She would have liked this quote from Buddha:

> *If you know anything that's hurtful and untrue, don't say it. If you know anything that's helpful and untrue, don't say it. If you know anything that is hurtful and true, don't say it. If you know anything that is helpful and true, find the right time.*

I've seen the concept of finding the right time work well for good corporate leaders. If you find the right time to say something, it generally works. If you say it at the wrong time, it can lead to confusion or hostility. The best way to improve your timing is to improve your listening. That way, you know what is on the mind of the other person. You can pick your moment. Good communicators find the right time, stick to the truth and say positive things.

My grandmother had another favourite: 'First engage the brain, then open the mouth'. She would have liked us to follow this sequence before we speak:

- Think about it first.
- Make sure it is helpful.
- Say only what is true.

Conversations would be too slow if you went through this step by step every time before you opened your mouth, but if you adopt these as part of your mindset your communication will improve. Most of the time you will easily know if it is the right time to say it.

PICKING THE RIGHT TIME

How do you know it is the right time to say something? Here I am talking about important pieces of communication. The right time has come when the other person is agreeable to listening, and is quiet and focused. That's why in the business world people make appointments or attend meetings; it means everybody is expecting the communication to take place. If they just barged into each other's offices and made strong statements, soon the company would be in total chaos.

Making sure that the other person is in the right frame of mind to listen is critical, but you also need to share this frame of mind. If either of you is diverted or agitated, the communication is likely to miss. By the way, if what you have to say implies a criticism, make sure that in your mind you are convinced the other person will be helped by the criticism and can overcome the problem. Without this attitude, you risk putting too much emphasis on the criticism and creating a hurtful message.

Positive messages result mainly from your own positive attitudes. If you think 'They probably won't take any notice of me', you will mostly be right. But if you think 'They will listen', they almost always will.

TALK IS NOT CHEAP

> **If either of you is diverted or agitated, the communication is likely to miss.**

One expression that holds many back is 'Talk is cheap'. This implies that talk never does anything and that it is easy to do. This is so far from the truth. Talk is not cheap.

How many times have you asked your teenager to do something and they do it the wrong way? At work, how many times have you asked a colleague to prepare a proposal and they have produced the wrong thing? Is it necessarily always their fault? Perhaps they didn't understand your request; because you didn't get the message across.

It was obviously someone who knows nothing about communication who said, 'Talk is cheap'. Talk can be costly, particularly when people misinterpret what you say. Talk can reduce trust, decrease cooperation and undermine friendships. That's why you will do better at work and at home if your talk amounts to real communication.

MORE COMMONSENSE TIPS

Some other old-fashioned values will help your spoken communication. For example, avoid slander and gossip, and be wary of any form of backstabbing or setting people off against each other. These can have a boomerang effect, coming back to cause you trouble.

Exaggeration is a common error, hurting the credibility of the person who is a consistent exaggerator. It is generally based on a wish to make oneself more interesting, and this is how others see it. If you accept the truth that you *are* interesting, you will have no need to exaggerate.

I have seen workplaces where the culture is rotten with gossip. Often this has been encouraged by the leadership, who prefer to divide people rather than build teams. These so-called leaders are unreliable and often untruthful in their own communication. They should not be at the top. Their divisiveness breeds further division. Gossip breeds gossip. In these environments, when people have something to say to a specific person, they say it to someone else. Put this way, it seems stupid, and it is. It's tough if you are working in that environment because it is like an infection. One way to defend yourself from the infection of gossip is to think 'If this is worth saying, why not say it to the person it is about?.'

In summary, you will make more friends and be trusted much more by people if you:

- Use meaningful, positive speech.
- Use kind words.
- Be polite.
- Be truthful.
- Avoid slander and backstabbing.

It is important to say 'No' without hurting people or making them feel that you don't like them. Simple things like an invitation to a game of tennis or to come round to dinner are good examples. If you cannot go, don't give 'No' as your first response—it makes the other person feel deflated. Instead, begin your answer by saying: 'That sounds like a wonderful idea, but I have a meeting that night. Thank you for asking'. This answer leaves both of you feeling positive about the communication. One-word answers (particularly 'No') are generally about ten or twenty words too short.

Management guru Peter Drucker is praised for many things, but what comes through strongest to me is his commonsense. He seems to have more commonsense than most of us, and he uses it well. He often talks about the responsibility of executives, while others may think about the power they have. Peter Drucker is seen as the man who invented management as a discipline, if not a science.

In an interview for *Boss* magazine, November 2000, Drucker was asked what advice he would give young managers today and what he would stress as the most important issues for them to tackle in their work. His answers provide helpful life tips for us all:

- **Take information responsibility.** Every six months or so, ask yourself: What information do I need to do my job? From whom? When? And in what form? And what information do I owe? To whom? When? In what form? Then make sure that all your associates know, understand and accept this.
- **Take career responsibility.** Ask yourself, and know the answers to, these questions: What are my strengths? What do I do well? What are my values? What are my limitations? What can I not do at all? Then you will have to learn where you belong, what your contribution could and should be and where you don't belong, and place yourself accordingly.
- **Build continuous learning into your life and work.** The assumption has to be that everybody who has not learned and relearned every three or four years has become obsolete, none more quickly than the people at the top. Learning does not necessarily involve going back to school, though that will be needed in many cases.
- **Be able to work in a number of different roles.** These roles are as a boss (occasionally), responsible for the productivity and effectiveness of other people; as a subordinate, responsible for making the boss productive and effective as a team member; and, more and more often, as a partner and contractor, and as someone who works with partners and alliances.

Drucker has always been heavy on commonsense. Since 1954 he has been saying that we all need balance. He has advised management that their biggest job is balancing the short term against the long term, risk against opportunity and one objective against another. His words really count for our personal lives. I think Drucker's contribution to my own understanding of communication is simply that, to be effective communicators, we need balance. If your mind is well balanced (positive not negative, relaxed not agitated) you will find that good communication follows.

> ... to be effective communicators, we need balance.

Business communication courses take many different approaches to help executives get the message across, but some things that keep coming up are:

- **Listen more than you talk.** This needs to be a quick decision; the moment a thought arises that would normally lead to words, hold it back and listen for a change.
- **Ask open questions starting with 'how'.** We usually feel on the defensive when asked the 'Why' question but we feel part of the team if people ask us 'How?' or 'What?' questions.

- **Be more informative and less opinionated.** People who quickly say 'No, that won't work' generally get nowhere. The problem stays unsolved and things that were bad get worse.
- **Give praise where it is due.** Praise is generally due much more often than you think, so communicate better by increasing the number of times you describe what a colleague did and exactly why it helped.

Researchers are finding that positive communication and a friendly environment are among the main reasons people stay with or leave a company. Surely this applies even more at home or in the community. If people do not feel appreciated, why would they stay in a job or club, or remain your friend or partner? If you have forgotten how to praise people, here are phrases to commit to memory and promise to use more often: thank you; well done; that was good; congratulations; terrific teamwork; what a good solution; that happened quicker than I thought it would; you have improved; didn't we have fun?; that was the best; great job; I'm glad you got that out of the way; yes, good idea; I like that; top effort; good result; great try; you'll do it.

27 YOU CAN BE A CREATIVE COMMUNICATOR

Working in a creative industry, I have heard so many people say 'I just can't be creative' or 'I wish I could produce creative ideas too'. The reality is you can increase your creativity by learning some of the tricks of the creative professionals. Creativity is a skill, just as communication is a skill. We tend to think people are born communicators, or born creators, but with few exceptions most have worked hard to get to their current level.

> **Creativity is in every part of life.**

I believe everyone can be creative. It is not just about producing a great film, a terrific advertisement or a new law of physics. Sure, these are creative acts. But you need to be creative at work and at home to increase your effectiveness and to have fun. Creativity is in every part of life. Your creativity may produce a new way for the family to have fun together or a new approach for the sporting club. It can be about solving old problems in new ways.

WAYS TO UNLOCK YOUR CREATIVITY

Being creative sure makes for better communication, so it is worth making the effort to unlock your creativity. Here are some tips.

Rebuild an open mind

When we were kids everything was new and we had an open way of looking at things. Gradually we've lost that childlike wonder and curiosity. It's worth trying to get some of it back as you become more open and more creative. If you bring a free and open mind to a problem or situation, you will be the first to spot the solution. Everyone else will be lost in their thoughts, bound down by the restrictive adult brain. So, a good start on the creative pathway is to think more as a kid.

Don't censor yourself

One of my colleagues had a great knack in business meetings. He would be the one who would say 'I know this is a dumb question, but . . .' and then ask the very question that was on everyone's mind but no-one else was game enough to ask. We don't ask these dumb questions because our mind acts as a censor. It says 'You should know' or 'They will laugh at you'. If your mind considers something and tells you 'That's silly', you may just have a creative idea in there, so ignore your mind and be prepared to take risks.

Move on from mistakes

I watched a creative team of art director and copywriter working on an advertising campaign. They had pieces of paper all over the place, a whiteboard full of scribbling and sheets stuck on every bit of wall space. Some of the words or ideas were clearly just ridiculous. As they talked, one or the other would come up with a lousy line or a weak joke. This did not stop them. They did not fear mistakes, they just ploughed right on.

Keep active, be involved

Creativity needs feeding, and the best food is the wonderful diversity of human life. To keep your creative energies growing, get out of the chair. See a movie. If you must watch TV, watch something you would normally reject. Buy a different magazine. Stroll through a shop with nothing in mind. Buy the latest CD from your least favourite singer. Don't keep closing more and more doors on the outside world; start to smash some of them open. The boss of a leading fund manager competes in triathlons on the weekends, because it stretches him physically and mentally into uncharted territory. He doesn't win, but he's not afraid of losing.

> *Don't keep closing more and more doors on the outside world...*

Leave things alone

Sometimes you need to get up from the desk, walk away and not come back to the issue for a while. Let it just percolate away in the back of your mind, because the mind in a relaxed state is great at producing answers. 'Let's sleep on that' is good advice.

Act on the idea

Once the creativity arises, you have then to put it to work. Pass it on, write it down, take the action, whatever. If you don't take action, the creativity can be lost. So share the idea with friends or colleagues, send it off in a memo, commit it to paper—or take any action that commits the creativity to memory.

TAKE A COMMUNICATION SKILLS COURSE

To get ahead today, you need more than technical or professional skills. You need to be more than a well-read lawyer, more than a competent plumber and more than a creative architect—you also need to be able to get the message across. Skills without communication amount to little today, but combine skills and communication and you have the keys to success. Even in sports, the most successful sporting figures are more than athletes, they are also good, highly trained communicators.

More companies are making it clear that the people they want to promote are those who have good communication skills. Just look in the senior appointments section of any newspaper and you will see that employers are expecting top communication skills from their top people. A fear of talking and relating will hold your career back, unless you take a communication skills course. This applies across the employment field. For doctors, plumbers, accountants, pilots, builders, architects, teachers, nurses, lawyers, shopkeepers and IT experts, communication is important to success and achievement.

It is also vital for those who want to get more out of community involvement and leadership. This is where good communication skills become a real differentiator, and you can see instant results from learning.

Communication is not a science; it is something you have to get out there and do, learning a little as you go. There probably are some natural communicators, but not many. Most good communicators have learnt new skills along the way. Almost every person we call a 'born communicator' has worked hard on communication skills. Most of us have to build continuous learning into our life, so why not make communication part of this learning? Perhaps your best time to pick up new communication skills is after you have been in the workplace for some time, say two to five years.

> ... combine skills and communication and you have the keys to success.

Paul, a leading corporate adviser, told me what his firm is doing as part of its recruiting program. To check out the real written communication skills of the applicant (as opposed to the slick CV), without warning they asked recruits to complete a short written exercise during the interview. This sorted a few out straight away (they left) while providing a positive pressure situation for the others.

To communicate better and get ahead, you may need real 'back to basics' learning, such as core aspects of writing (including grammar, punctuation and spelling). Such a skills course could also include preparation of documents, making presentations, speaking to small and large groups, plus negotiation skills. For the more advanced, better relationships and career prospects come from learning team communication, conflict resolution, intercultural communication and interviewing skills.

If you doubt the importance of communication, go back to those job advertisements in the newspapers. Most will actually say that the employer is looking for good communication, such as the ability to write, work in teams and sell the message to others.

Once you get the job, decisions about how far to promote you up the corporate ladder are based even more on how well you have communicated within the organisation. Many times chief executives have asked me, as their communication adviser, how well someone in their organisation communicates. Almost always this happens when promotion is being considered. I have also consulted to many businesspeople when they were second in charge, aiming for the top job. These business leaders knew the important role communication would play in their success, so they started early in polishing their speaking skills, adding persuasion to their communication and authority to their messages.

A number of surveys show that computer professionals climb the corporate ladder more slowly than people from marketing, finance and even from production. The reason? As a group, the computer professionals were often seen as 'unresponsive, expressionless and extremely self-controlled'. Their employers did not want to put them in positions where relating to people really mattered, and so their careers stalled.

The beauty about learning good communication is that you win in two ways: you'll be more likely to get ahead and you will be happier. So, while you contemplate your career or relationships and how well they are going, ask yourself: how long since you attended a communication course? It's your move.

BE CREATIVE, BE HAPPY

Becoming creative is not necessarily about become another Einstein or Picasso. If you lock into your own creative juices, you will become more fun, more interesting, happier and more of a contributor. Overall, that makes you a better communicator.

We are living in great times, creative times. Look at the great changes we have been through. Think about the wonderful opportunities ahead. Times are changing fast. Knowledge is exploding. We can talk to anybody, anywhere, at any time. We can also transact most of our business anywhere, anyhow, at any time. Nothing seems impossible.

Our sense of community is our strongest defence against those who promote fear and terror. Being free allows us to communicate; communicating makes us free. Open communication is the enemy of the dictator, the oppressor.

While we remember those in the world who do not have our privileges, let's commit to use our good fortune well. Let's commit to creating a world where everything works well for everybody. Let's move on from the idea that for one person to win somebody else must lose. Even corporations are moving on from seeing business

> **Let's move on from the idea that for one person to win somebody else must lose.**

as a battleground. Now they're looking for friends and partners.

Nothing is impossible. The optimists can win. So let's be inspired. Let's get on with life. We can create the future. We can belong. We can put real value on everybody, not just those at the top. A sense of community will make this century great. The human spirit can make it different. Without communication there is no community, so by starting now, you can improve your communication and your community. Ultimately, this local action will build a global community.

Dream a little, do a lot. Small moments of magic can add up to a great life. Your mind can be controlled and at peace. Let's wipe out the fear of failure so ideas can flourish. Get out of your seats. Talk to someone. Talk to your family. We can be happy. The future awaits: what are you going to do?

INDEX

action 6, 29, 56, 115
adoption, of product 36
adoption process 35–6
advertising 10, 34, 39, 105, 113–14, 182
  slogans 17, 106
agenda setting 30, 44, 144
aggression 120–1
Alafaci, Dominic 14
Ali, Muhammed 154
Alpha course 182
analytical listening 105
anger 91–100, 103, 142
  dealing with 92–3
apologising 98–9
Aristotle 65
article writing 14
assertiveness 122–4
attitude 18, 24, 54, 120
audience, primary/secondary 4
audience research 7–8, 33, 58, 154–5
awareness, of new product 35–6

balance 188
benchmarking 20
Bernays, Edward L. 7–9, 55–6
blaming 114, 179–80
body language 17, 158
  positive 56–7
bosses 53, 64
brainstyles 58–60
  the conceptor 59
  the conciliator 58, 59
  the deliberator 59
  the knower 58, 59
Brainstyles: Change Your Life

Without Changing Who You Are 58
brand experience 181–2
brand image 36–8, 48
brand loyalty
  differentiators 160–1
  people are key 160–1, 165–6
brevity 43–4
bullying 46
bunker mentality 113
business briefs 136
business development 10–11
buzz, creating 15–16

calmness 126, 127
career advancement 53, 82–3, 110, 192
  and email 167
  and networking 47, 49, 50
  responsibility for 188
Carnegie, Dale 41
categorisation, of people 58–60, 62
cause-related marketing 49–50
centres of influence 11–12, 13
change 18–20, 30, 85, 112
  survival tips 108–10
channel, of communication 115, 173
cheating 5
clarity 32–3, 86, 141
common ground 77, 144, 169
commonsense 86, 162, 187, 188
communication 28, 39, 78, 177–9
  barriers 19, 20–1
  defined 20, 177

195

INDEX

effective 17, 21, 32, 38, 61–5, 188
face-to-face 34
global 17, 18
improving 21, 64, 192
intangible results 34, 50, 68
interpersonal 17–18, 76
key to success 10–11
mirages 68–9
negative 18, 30, 91, 121
poor 5, 6, 106
seven strategies 12
three-step process 66, 72–4
total package 14
training in 21–2, 23
communication balance sheet 63–4
communication block 39–40
communication breakdown 20, 70, 101–2, 113–18
dealing with 116–17
communication divide 19
communication review 23
communication skills 17, 18, 23, 25, 27, 91, 165
community 18, 49, 50, 65, 87, 159, 180, 192, 193, 194
competence 11, 22, 76
complaints 18
compliments 18
compromise 76–7
conclusions, jumping to 21
conferences 15, 41, 44, 45
confidence 22, 44, 45, 136, 137
conflict 119–20
conflict management 116, 120–4
confusion 4, 6, 21, 32, 105
consistency, of message 3, 173
continuous learning 188, 192
control 128–9
conversations 63, 70, 111, 117, 171, 178–9
celebrating the mundane 72
cooperation 18, 26, 62, 81–2
corporate anger 94–5

problem solving 95–8
corporate communication 3, 18, 53
corporate image 5, 6
corporate mind 17
corporate PR, effective 84–5, 87–8
agility 85
commonsense 86
focus 85–6
promotion 86–7
relationships 87
correspondence *see* letter writing
courage 20, 26, 87, 146
courses, in communication skills 16, 191–3
creativity 26, 56, 190–1, 193–4
credibility 14, 29, 77
credibility killers, for women 79–82
crisis communication 111–12
crisis management 116–17
criticism 18
culture, of workplace 15, 19, 79
curiosity 74, 83, 190
customer service 181–2
customers 5, 25, 40, 61–2, 113
always right 161–2
broader definition 159
dissatisfied 38, 114, 171, 181
satisfied 182
cynicism 36

decision, to change 19
dependence 4
dialogue 105, 110, 178
differences, personal 58–60, 69
DiResta, Diane 79–82
disclosure, fear of 94, 95, 173
dramatisation 77
dress, appropriate 81
Drucker, Peter 111, 187–8

e-commerce 168
e-communication 170–4

INDEX

ego 25, 126, 171
emails 15, 167, 170, 174
 with power 168–70
 subject title 168
emotion 37, 126, 144, 154, 169
empathetic listening 105
empathy 76, 77, 131
endorsement 14
enjoyment 76
enthusiasm 76
environment policy 19, 20
Epictetus 5
ethics 19, 20, 29
evaluation, of product 36
exaggeration 71–2, 164, 187
eye contact 56, 57, 73, 123, 137–8, 147, 158

facts 71, 77, 96, 111, 116, 169
failure 66–7, 73, 92, 120–1, 159
fear 5, 20, 78
 of communicating 3, 7, 21–2, 25, 39, 49, 56, 75, 104
 of disclosure 94, 95, 173
 of meetings 144–5
 of new people 53, 64
 'note it, ignore it' technique 54
 overcoming 23–7
 positive energy 54–5
 of public speaking 151–3
 of rejection 55
feedback 36, 70, 124, 149
 in negotiation 128
 in presentations 137
 in selling 165
feelings *see* emotion
financial planners 10–12
Financial Planning Association (FPA) 14
first impressions 57
five Ws, of opening a meeting 83
flexibility 75–6, 77, 85

focus 43, 85–6
Foley, Elizabeth 46–7
follow-up 45
Ford, intranet 167–8
freedom 39, 40, 193
Freud, Sigmund 7
friendliness 24, 44, 56
friends 18, 45, 58, 61, 63
 in boxes 62
 corporate 4
 making 53–4, 55–6, 64–5
 segmenting 4, 6
 valuing 40
functions 41, 44, 45, 53, 146–9

Gallup Organisation 117, 160, 161, 166
 StrengthsFinder system 129–31
gestures 81, 158
giving 126
glass ceiling 78, 79
globalisation 18
goal setting 44
Goldhaber Research Associates 167
good causes 49–50
gossip 5, 109, 114, 186–7
Gray, Malcolm 154
Guidance Paper on Presentation Skills 157
guiding listening 105

happiness 41, 46, 50, 57, 59, 65, 107, 165
 achieving 183–4
 in business presentations 136–7
 and creativity 193–4
 defined 182–3
 happy face 34, 35
 and negotiation 127–8
happiness principle 69–72
Harkins, Philip J. 117
Harvard Business School 122

head nodding   80
Hill and Knowlton   19, 20
honesty   20, 32, 70, 74, 77, 164
hostility   110–11, 119
How to Win Friends and Influence People   41
human spirit   177–81, 183, 194
humanity   178
hypocrisy   120

ideas, credit for   81
ignorance   22
image   20, 28
imagination   75
impact   83, 129–30
influence   8, 53–4, 128–9
information, responsibility for   188
information flow, to media   31
information technology   22, 167
   see also Internet; website skills
Inglehart, Ronald   178
interest
   creating   71, 77
   in new product   36
Internet   18, 61, 63, 168, 170, 174
   and communication   167
   interactive websites   56
interruptions   80, 126–7
intranet, at Ford   167–8
introductions   44–5
involvement   25, 50, 65, 137, 191

joke telling   150, 156

key people, cultivating   8, 9
Kirner, Joan   47–8
Kotex   162

language
   modifiers   80
   simple   82
   tag lines   80
   uptalk   80
   see also speaking skills
Lasker, Albert   162
lateral thinking   8, 12, 136, 162
leadership   28, 79, 81–2, 84–7, 117
   and email   167
Lee, Ivy Ledbetter   95
legal action   94
letter writing   15, 38–9
Levine, Rick   173
Lewis, Fulton Jr   26
life themes   129–31
   impacting   129–30
   relating   130–1
listening   39, 47, 188
   in negotiation   126–7
   three types   105
   and timing   185
   vital skill   35, 37, 73, 143
Locke, Christopher   173
loneliness   4
Longstaff, Simon   179–80
love   5, 37, 48–9, 180, 183
loyalty   11, 75, 76
lying   114, 163

McEwen, Dr Bill   160, 161
Mackay, Hugh   47
management style, collaborative   80, 82
Managing in a Time of Great Change   111
manipulation   8–9, 30
mannerisms   158
market research   5, 21, 69, 97, 104
marketing   37, 61
marketplaces   171
mass communication   17
mass marketing   62
Meaning At Work   183
media   29
   training tips   31
   using   5–6, 14
   see also radio

meetings 81, 140–5, 167
  asking for questions 142
  contributions 142, 143
  objectives 143
  purpose 140, 143
memorability 8
messages 17, 22, 61, 106
  boring 26, 169
  clear 32–3, 141
  consistent 3, 173
  happy 34
  line of the day 29–30
  positive 186
  powerful 32–3
  prepared 82
  tailoring 7–8, 61, 69–70, 71, 77, 169
  targeted 127, 165
  timing of 8, 20, 21, 31, 135, 185–6
  unwanted 104–5
  using experts 8
  using themes 72–3, 86
Miller, Marlane 58
mind 53
  angry 92
  balanced 188
  chattering 54, 164
  open 190
  power of 17, 23–4, 27, 53–4, 91, 116
  see also monkey mind
mistakes 71, 191
modesty 15
monkey mind 7, 23, 24, 91, 92, 127, 152
Myers-Briggs type indicators 58

names 41, 43
  how to remember 42
National Committee for a Free Europe 25–6
needs 36, 164
neglect 15
negotiation 125–9
  and sales 163–4
nervousness 25, 53, 153
  see also fear
networking 11–12, 13, 46–50, 77, 149
  after-hours 65
  and careers 47
  internal 47
  in new situations 64–5
  personality types 48–9
  tips 42–5, 65
networks 46, 48
new ideas, barriers to communicating 117–18

Ogilvy on Advertising 57
Ogilvy, David 57
one-on-one discussion 114
openness 20, 24, 26, 27, 44, 62
organisations
  happiness principle 69–72
  successful 34–5

Page, Arthur W. 25–6
Parker and Lee 95
participation, in seminars/functions 13–14, 15
parties 146–9
partnerships 5, 12, 62, 128
patience 27, 30, 35, 40, 65, 98, 100
people
  being interested in 5, 21, 25, 35, 41, 43, 77, 78
  categorising 58–60, 62
  concern for 25, 35, 69–70, 78, 107
  importance of 10, 160–1, 165–6
  influencing 53–4
  introducing 44–5
  liking them 5, 6, 40, 56, 74
perceptions 4–5, 6, 20, 22, 43, 82, 97
performance 5–6, 63

perseverance 70, 72, 77, 87
persistence *see* perseverance
personality 48–9
personality types 58–60
perspective 92, 93, 135
persuasion 33, 75, 76–8, 169, 170
policy making 19–20
politicians 28, 43
posture 81
power 128–30
Powerful Conversations: How High Impact Leaders Communicate 117
praise 188
precision 43–4
preoccupation 66, 67
presentations 13, 33, 135–9
 concluding 138
PricewaterhouseCoopers 183
primary audience 4
probing 136
problem solving 109
 corporate 95–8
problems 93, 108, 121
Proctor & Gamble 105
profile 14
promotion (in career) 14, 75–6, 84, 169, 192, 193
 and women 78–82
public relations 34–5, 84, 113–14
Public Relations Consultants Association (UK) 157
public speaking 14, 54–5, 81–2, 150–8
 handling questions 110, 158
 how not to 150–1
 Public Speaking 154
 stage fright 151–3
purpose 83
pushovers 99–100

question and answer sessions 110, 158

questioning 37, 44, 73
 and listening 105
 in selling 160
 vital skill 13, 35, 40, 56, 70, 83, 106
questions
 in emails 169
 open-ended 44, 188

radio, for publicity 14, 87
Rasman, Tony 116
Ray, Greg 19
Rayner, Moira 47–8
Reagan, Ronald 29, 156
referrals 11
rejection 55, 56, 91
 planning for 55
relationships 10, 49, 56, 62, 63
 disputes 112
 failed 4
 with influential people 8, 9
 insecurity 47
 need for communication 36
 protection/connection 87
repetition 30, 35, 41, 70, 73, 82, 86, 154
resentment 91–2, 100, 103
responsibility 188
Rinpoche, Tulku Thondup 93
Robbins, Steven 115
Roberts, Kevin 37, 48, 49, 180–1
Rogen International 125, 126, 136, 167
roles, at work 188
rumours 114

Saatchi & Saatchi 37, 63, 178
sales communication 159–66
salespeople 159–60
SAP, B2E communication 168
Schmidt, Eric 170
Searls, Doc 173
self-assessment 19
self-esteem 23, 39, 72

self-image   25, 40, 49
self-knowledge   3, 6, 82
self-liking   4, 6, 23, 46, 184
self-obsession   135, 165
self-promotion   14, 75, 76, 79, 107
selfishness   101–7
  overcoming   102–4
selling   45, 61, 159–66
  patter   163
seminars   13–14, 44, 45
separateness, in negotiation   126
shyness   23, 24, 71
silence   66–7, 73, 107, 115–16
Silverstein, Michael   181
sincerity   137
smiling   56, 57, 79, 143, 145, 147, 152
social gatherings   146–9
speaking skills   80, 186–7
  speaking up   81
  talking 'down'   115
  uptalk   80
  voice control   81, 157–8
Spector and Associates Inc.   56
speech   185
speeches, presidential   33
speechmaking *see* public speaking
spirit
  defined   177
  see also human spirit
Springboard   182
stage fright   151–3
strangers   53, 54
StrengthsFinder system   129–31
stress management   31–2, 104
support   18, 64, 87

talking   18, 26, 186
  too much   104–7
tangibility, of message   5–6
teamwork   78, 144
Telstra   4, 5

Terez, Tom   183
The Boston Consulting Group   181
The Cluetrain Manifesto: The End of Business as Usual   173
The Good Listener   47
The Healing Power of Mind   93
The Women's Power Handbook   47
thinking
  creative   8, 12, 136, 162
  positive   93
Tibetan Buddhism   182–3
timing   8, 20, 21, 31, 135, 185–6
tit for tat reactions   122
trade shows   15
trial, of product   36
trust   20, 63, 77
Turnbull Porter Novelli   4, 5
Twain, Mark   151

uptalk   80

victim mentality   91, 110
visualisation   7, 26, 42, 55, 104, 120, 144–5
voice control   81, 157–8
vulnerability audit   19

Watson Wyatt   183
website skills   56, 170–3
Weinberger, David   173
Western Mining Corporation (WMC)   20
women
  credibility killers, at work   79–82
  and promotion   78–82
workshops   13–14
World Wide Web *see* Internet
writing skills   192
written communication   15, 38–9

Yates, Sandra   63, 178